Holy Ground

Prior Publications by Julie K. Aageson

One Hope: Re-Membering the Body of Christ (Augsburg Fortress and Liturgical Press, 2015) (Co-authored in commemoration of the 500th anniversary of the Protestant Reformation)

Benedictions: 26 Reflections (Wipf and Stock, 2016)

HOLY GROUND

An Alphabet of Prayer

Julie K. Aageson

CASCADE *Books* · Eugene, Oregon

HOLY GROUND
An Alphabet of Prayer

Cascade Books
An Imprint of Wipf and Stock Publishers
199 W. 8th Ave., Suite 3
Eugene, OR 97401

www.wipfandstock.com

PAPERBACK ISBN: 978-1-5326-3922-7
HARDCOVER ISBN: 978-1-5326-3923-4
EBOOK ISBN: 978-1-5326-3924-1

Cataloguing-in-Publication data:

Names: Aageson, Julie K.

Title: Holy ground : an alphabet of prayer / Julie K. Aageson

Description: Eugene, OR: Cascade Books, 2018 | Includes bibliographical refer-
ences.

Identifiers: ISBN 978-1-5326-3922-7 (paperback) | ISBN 978-1-5326-3923-4
(hardcover) | ISBN 978-1-5326-3924-1 (ebook)

Subjects: LCSH: Prayer—Christianity | Spiritual life—Christianity

Classification: BV2010.3 A132 2018 (paperback) | BV2010.3 (ebook)

Manufactured in the U.S.A.   12/29/17

With love and gratitude for my three daughters, Erin Kristine, Anne Elizabeth, and Megan Kathleen, each of whom is woven into these reflections in subtle and not so subtle ways. Their presence in my life is holy ground.

Contents

Permissions

Enthusiasm, p. 20. Use of the lines from "Now the feast and celebration, all of creation sings for joy." Haugen, "Now the Feast." 1990, GIA. Fair use.

Enthusiasm, p. 20. Use of the line, "This is the feast of victory for our God." *Evangelical Lutheran Worship*, Augsburg Fortress, 2006. Fair use.

Faith, p. 24. "O God, Why are You Silent." Text by Marty Haugen. GIA, 2003. All rights reserved. Used with permission.

Nurturing, p. 57. "Mothering God, You Gave Me Birth." Text by Jean Janzen. Minneapolis, Augsburg Fortress, 1995. Used with permission.

Yearning, p. 104. "Christ, Be Our Light" ©1993, Bernadette Farrell. Published by Oregon Catholic Press. 5536 NE Hassalo, Portland, OR 97213 All rights reserved. Used with permission.

Yearning, p. 105. Use of the lines ". . . for peace in the world, for the health of the church, for the unity of all . . . for peace in our hearts, for peace in our homes . . . let us pray to the Lord." *Evangelical Lutheran Worship*, Augsburg Fortress, 2006. Reproduced with permission.

Preface

When I was very young, I learned to pray in all the places young children are wont to do. There were the usual prayers before meals—*Come Lord Jesus, be our guest, let these gifts to us be blessed* and *O give thanks to the Lord for God is good and God's mercy endures forever*—prayed with one eye half open in order better to survey the food before us. Sometimes prayer followed the meal—*Thanks dear Lord, for meat and drink, through Jesus Christ, Amen*—said in a cadence that resembled marching, which might have been what we wished we were doing, eager as we were to get away from the table and on to more interesting things.

And there were bedtime prayers, these more complicated and often more engaging if only because they were a way of prolonging evenings spent with parents at our bedside—*Now I lay me down to sleep. I pray dear Lord my soul to keep. If I should die before I wake, I pray dear Lord my soul to take.* I don't remember conversations about death, though this prayer certainly could have opened a door into a long night of interesting questions. *Dear Jesus, be with all the people behind the Iron Curtain. Protect everyone behind the Bamboo Curtain and be with those surrounded by the Wall. Watch over all the hungry children in China* . . . These images conveyed all sorts of possibilities for nighttime conversation. What was that iron curtain actually made of and how did bamboo become a curtain? Was *everyone* behind some sort of wall or barrier? Might walls—barriers—mean something more than physical dividers or ramparts? How, really, could we share our food? And might food also be a metaphor for other kinds of nourishment?

Later on, I remember the prayers of my mother and father, and especially those of my grandparents, whose habits of prayer helped shape the whole family. I also recall conversations about how to pray and how not to pray. These were not necessarily analytical or systematic reviews of types of prayer as much as critiques of people who prayed in ways thought—perhaps only by us—to be self-serving or manipulative or lacking understanding of a God who did not serve as our divine and personal valet, delivering weather we requested or answers we sought or any other exchange of prayer for goods.

When a well-meaning friend might tell of praying for rain for her garden and another neighbor about hoping it wouldn't rain while his cherry orchard was vulnerable and rain would mean cracked fruit, the irony was not lost on us. What would God do? Who would God decide to please? Deep down, we knew that our prayers were not about bargaining with God and not about exchanging conversation and information with the sacred—as if God only needed to know more in order to respond appropriately.

Even at a young age, perhaps because of the experience of prayer in worship, we knew prayer to be about putting ourselves in places where God might be present. I also had a keen sense of being *with* God, experiencing the sacred in daily life, and knowing that somehow this too is prayer—mysterious, enigmatic, inexplicable, both knowing and not knowing.

Later as a young adult, I discovered the writings of a great rabbi, Abraham Joshua Heschel, who introduced me to a Jewish sensibility: God resting on our eyelids. I loved the immediacy and literalness of the image coupled with Heschel's passionate belief that God accompanies us whether we desire God's presence or not.

I also remember a story—perhaps told by Rabbi Heschel—of a Jewish shoemaker who would work late into the evening repairing the worn shoes of fellow villagers, the only pair of shoes they owned, so that they could return to work the following morning. The poor shoemaker found himself torn between making time to pray the required daily prayers of his tradition and repairing the shoes so desperately needed by his customers. His sigh of frustration became a prayer, a literal longing for God to be present in his work of mending and sewing and repairing—in order for the people of his village to wear shoes the next day. The sigh of the shoemaker was enough.

Too often we turn prayer into well-intentioned patterns of our own making. Too often we assume prayer is primarily about words. Sometimes there's an almost magical understanding that if we get the words right, if we trust enough, if we believe enough, God will answer. But most of us know that God is not a divine magician and that prayer is much more than our feeble attempts to make God pay attention to what God already knows *or* to make of God a puppet responding to our tugs on the strings of God's heart. Prayer is so much more than words.

Several years ago, I was invited to write a monthly column for a denominational magazine. I was at once both honored and terrified. The column's title, *Let Us Pray*, conveyed certain assumptions I was not at all sure about—did they think I had prayer all figured out? Did they assume I was a disciplined pray-er, perhaps one of those "prayer warriors" I'd heard about? Did they have any idea how much I struggle with praying, with knowing how to talk to God, listen to God? Did they know of my doubts and skepticism about much of Christian life?

I wanted to write and I wanted to write about all I do not know. The editors said yes and we were off and running. After some years of columns which seemed to resonate with readers, I chose to use the alphabet as a template for the monthly articles. It provided a pattern to follow for twenty-six columns. It fit the allotted months ending appropriately in December almost three years later. And it allowed me to write about an expansive and spacious understanding of prayer, ways of praying that might not include words.

Armed with a large assortment of books on prayer and an especially lovely tome by Frederic and Mary Ann Brussat, *Spiritual Literacy: Reading the Sacred in Everyday Life*, I set out to explore prayer and spiritual practices alphabetically, following many of their suggestions as ways for understanding prayer in everyday life. I also paid attention to the writings of Richard Rohr and his admonition that prayer is not primarily words but a place, an attitude, a stance—and that for Jesus, prayer seems to be a matter of waiting in love, returning to love, and trusting that love is the unceasing stream of reality.[1]

The prayers I learned as a child were bookmarked by Scripture: daily readings, family devotions, worship. Because I am steeped in the rich biblical traditions of a liturgical church, patterns of biblical prayer are rooted in my psyche. Early on, I found the stories of the Bible to be multilayered, complex, enigmatic—a way of listening to a mysterious God. Over the years, these encounters with Scripture continue to challenge and engage. Listening to God in Scripture is part of my habit, part of my history. But *Holy Ground: An Alphabet of Prayer* is not meant to be a theological or biblical description of prayer. *Holy Ground* reflects some non-traditional ways of thinking about the spirit of the living God and how God's spirit might be heard in ways or places or acts often not associated with prayer. This book reveals my wrestling with a God who makes the ordinary holy. "Cleave the wood and I am there," says Isaiah in the apocryphal Gospel of Thomas. "Lift up the stone, and you will find me there."

Those twenty-six columns written for *GATHER*, revised and rewritten for book format, are the basis of *Holy Ground: An Alphabet of Prayer*. Readers will find here a collection of reflections about prayer as **A**ttention, **B**eauty, **C**ompassion, **D**evotion, **E**nthusiasm, **F**aith, **G**ratitude, **H**ospitality, **I**magination, **J**oy, **K**indness, **L**istening, **M**indfulness, **N**urturing, **O**penness, **P**lay, **Q**uesting, **R**everence, **S**tillness, **T**hanksgiving, **U**nity, **V**ision, **W**onder, **X** signifying mystery, **Y**earning, and **Z**eal. This alphabet is one way of thinking about the practice of prayer in broader, more inclusive language *and* practice. It's meant to help readers experience prayer as the sigh of the shoemaker, too busy to drop his worn shoes and

---

1. From Rohr, "Becoming Pure in Heart." https://cac.org/becoming-pure-heart-2016-05-11/.

kneel in disciplined prayer but not too busy to recognize and acknowledge God's presence in the midst of ordinary life. And it's
meant to celebrate prayer in the broadest of ways as together with
all of humanity we yearn to know God and to be known by God.

Each reflection begins alphabetically with beautifully formed
calligraphic letters. These pages are meant to encourage engagement with that particular word: a place for meditation, reflection,
and should it "suit the reader's fancy", coloring or embellishing
the letters. In this way, readers are invited to practice God's presence meditatively and perhaps tangibly in the pleasure of coloring
or embellishing the designated words for prayer. Following each
reflection, readers are encouraged to consider their own ways
of praying using a statement and questions for pondering God's
presence: paying **attention** to daily life, looking for **beauty** in the
commonplace, showing **compassion**, practicing **devotion**, celebrating **enthusiasm**—all the way to discovering **wonder**, the X as
mystery, and the Z as **zeal** for a God who continues to pursue us
in our everyday lives. It is the hope of the author that these simple
acts of creating and contemplating will connect readers to the holy
ground of everyday prayer—from **A** to **Z**.

Julie K. Aageson

ATTENTION

Attention

"Listen up!" I used to say to my students and later on to my daughters. "Let me see your eyes." I wanted their complete attention, their ears *and* their eyes. I expected them to stop what they were doing and focus on what was about to be shared. I wanted them to be present and to take notice. Giving one's attention to something implies courtesy and consideration, perhaps even thoughtfulness and responsiveness. Attention is a way of being present, a form of prayer.

Several years ago I was invited to write a monthly column for a denominational magazine. The invitation was a surprise and I was both honored and a bit frightened at the prospect of writing about a spiritual practice I did not claim to understand or do particularly well. I could recall the faithful prayers of my grandparents, those regular devotional times around the tables of my growing up, prayers said routinely at bedtime and mealtime, and prayers for specific situations and people. But this invitation to the holy ground of prayer required careful and honest attention.

Layered on top of that insecurity were the deeper issues of what prayer is, how prayer is practiced, and an all-too-ubiquitous understanding of prayer as an exchange of ideas or a list of requests or a private means of accessing God. I had always found deep meaning in the prayers of the liturgy and corporate worship. If I could somehow define prayer as paying attention, listening for God's voice in others and in the ordinary events of daily life, I could write honestly and authentically—even in a monthly magazine with regular deadlines.

As my narrower understanding of prayer became more expansive, I began to pay attention to God's presence in less linear and carefully defined ways. Perhaps it was related to becoming a mother and finding ways to pray—to *be*—in the midst of endlessly long days and too many sleepless nights. Or perhaps it was a lifelong awareness of the mystery of God's presence, inexplicably compelling, irritatingly tenacious, a perpetual mindfulness that demanded attention.

Prayer became for me a way of looking at the world—a place, an attitude, a stance; not so much an action as the living presence of God within us. Possibly that is what it was all along. But the common definitions which seemed to me what others more disciplined and pious called prayer were not often my experience.

Do you remember a children's television program called *Mr. Roger's Neighborhood*? Fred Rogers was a tall, lanky fellow whose soft voice and ways of paying attention to the smallest things were not easily forgotten. In contrast to a lot of children's programs or to almost everything else that seeks to demand our attention, Mr. Rogers invited children and adults to notice things: a warm sweater he donned at the beginning of each program, a neighbor who needed help, birds that welcomed food in the wintertime, flowers beginning to break through the soil to seek the warmth and light of the sun, a pair of sneakers that protected his feet, each of the children who watched his programs and what it was they were feeling that day—nearly 900 programs over several decades meant to help children pay attention.

Perhaps adults liked Mr. Rogers because they too wanted to pay attention. They recognized his regard for even the smallest things. Together with children whose eyes and ears sometimes notice and pay attention to things adults take for granted, Mr. Rogers methodically honored the world God has given us by paying attention.

Pay attention to the reflections in *Holy Ground: An Alphabet of Prayer*. They are invitations to think more broadly about the practice of prayer. Pay attention to all the ways God speaks and acts. Pay attention to praying without words, being present, practicing silence, listening. Pay attention to the holy ground where you are. Notice the world around you. See your place in the world with fresh eyes. Look and feel and listen to God's voice within you and within others. Attention—mindfulness—will help illuminate the living presence of God within us: much more, much beyond, and much closer than we sometimes think God to be. I hope this God who defies our paltry definitions and categories will continue to become the lens through which we see ourselves and this earth we call home.

Let us pray with our eyes and our ears and our hands. Let us take notice of one another, of the things we carry and bear. Help us attend to daily life, to the presence of ordinary rhythms and the extraordinary ways they convey God's love and grace. Help us honor the world and the holy ground where we live by being mindful, paying attention, being present. O God, make us attentive.

REFLECTION

Prayer became for me a way of looking at the world—a place, an attitude, a stance and not so much an action as the living presence of God within us. I want us to think about the deeper issues of what prayer is, how prayer is practiced, and an all-too-ubiquitous understanding of prayer as an exchange of ideas or a list of requests or a private means of accessing God.

- What are some ways you pay attention to God's presence in less linear and defined ways?
- How have your notions of prayer changed?
- How do you understand the view that attention—mindfulness—illuminates the living presence of God within us?
- Let us pray with our eyes and our ears and our hands. Let us take notice of one another, of the things we carry and bear. Name some ways you pay attention to praying without using words.

Beauty

Beauty

"EARTH IS CRAMMED WITH heaven and every common bush afire with God." Oh, Elizabeth Barrett Browning, how many times we've repeated your poetry and imagined ourselves in the lush green English countryside of your beautiful world. How many times your words have reminded us to pay attention to the beauty of our earth home, our own holy ground. Perhaps we have it backwards when we think of heaven as a place "out there." Swiss psychiatrist and psychoanalyst Carl Jung invites us to think of heaven and earth as a piece—the earth is in heaven. Human and spirit are not divided. Earth and heaven are one. Without ignoring or minimizing the brokenness and unspeakable suffering of our world, the beauty of this place we call home is among the most tangible ways we understand God.

Not long ago, my spouse and I spent an evening on the top of a mountain pass. Driving the long and circuitous road to get to the top of the pass, we watched the slow setting of the sun and the shadows of the mountains surrounding us as they slowly turned shades of rose and purple and then inky black. Finally darkness came and from the south we could see the international space station in its orbit, moving around the earth every ninety minutes. As it passed overhead, more and more stars began to appear and we could make out constellations and the obvious formations of the Big Dipper and Cassiopeia with its distinctive W shape. As midnight approached and the light of the western sky turned completely dark, our own Milky Way Galaxy began to show its unfathomable size and beauty just overhead. Through telescopes, we could see other galaxies including Andromeda as well as dying stars and "shooting stars" and stars just being born. Most of all, we gazed with wonder at the heavens above us and at the stars and planets and galaxies that silently blossomed across the fields of the night sky. In the stillness and awe of that night, we truly understood the earth to be in heaven.

The ancients lived in a world of daylight and darkness. Without artificial light and the endless daytime of our era in history, they experienced the wonder of the night and perhaps the humility of looking out into the cosmos that shaped their universe. They made gods of the stars and depended on their stories about them for making sense of daily life. I want to think about the extraordinary beauty of the universe as a way of speaking with God and sharing God's generativity and grace.

In the places where I live, we are surrounded by astonishing natural beauty. Ocean beaches and coastal mountain ranges, river gorges and volcanic peaks, endless varieties of flora and fauna, desert and forest, glacial lakes and craggy mountain foothills—none of which ever grows old. The beauty in these places is mind-boggling. My grandfather called this part of the world "Shangri-la"—his way of setting it apart and labeling it "earth crammed with heaven." Poetry and music, photography and painting don't begin to do justice to this handiwork of creation. Here in this place I find God's sacred presence and a sense of the wonder of my own life. In the places where I live and share the everyday ordinary rhythms of daily life, I see and hear and taste God's presence. Prayer indeed.

But of course there is beauty everywhere and each of us experiences beauty in thousands of different ways. Among the broken shards of the Gaza Strip, in the midst of hunger and water shortages and the unrelenting dehumanizing of the Palestinian people, a young shepherd boy plays a violin as he, like the pied piper he imagines himself to be, leads a flock of sheep out of the hills and back to their ragged and rocky stalls before the coming of night. In Aleppo and Paris and Beirut and Manchester, there is beauty in the faces of first responders and doctors and all those who risk their own lives to help others caught in cycles of violence and despair.

We pay attention to beauty as a way of praying. On Facebook recently, a friend posted a photo of an early morning sunrise. The picture was titled, "Begin with yes" reminding me of a reflection by twentieth-century psychiatrist Viktor Frankl. Frankl described being at work in a trench, the ravages of war dark and broken all around him. As he struggled to find the reason for such suffering and hopelessness, he sensed his spirit piercing through the gloom with a resounding *yes* in the face of what seemed to be a meaningless world. At the same time, a light came on in a distant farmhouse on the gray horizon affirming Frankl's *yes*, affirming God's *yes*.

O God, let us pray with eyes to see beauty and ears to hear music. Let us pray with our hands and our hearts so that beauty is not only what you give but what we make.

REFLECTION

Most of all, we gazed with wonder at the heavens above us and at the stars and planets and galaxies that silently blossomed across the fields of the night sky—prayer indeed.

- In the stillness and awe of that night, we truly understood the earth to be in heaven. How do you experience earth and heaven as one?
- To find beauty in the midst of horror and death seems strange. Yet Viktor Frankl's *yes* is an affirmation of God's presence in spite of so much darkness and suffering. What does it mean to you to begin with *yes*?
- Without ignoring or minimizing the brokenness and unspeakable suffering of our world, the beauty of this place we call home is among the most tangible ways we understand God. How is paying attention to beauty a way of praying for you?

Compassion

Compassion

Compassion as prayer? Compassion as a way of looking at the world, a habit, a lens for understanding God and the truth of God that is in each of us? Compassion as holy ground? Truth to tell, sitting as so many of us do in the midst of comfort and privileged lives in the first world, I'm uneasy writing about compassion. It falls a bit too easily off our lips. Its sound and its intent require too much of us. If we truly allow ourselves the spirit of compassion—the *cost* of compassion—our worlds surely will be turned upside down. Our hearts will be broken. Compassion is more than concern, more than empathy, much more than understanding and kindness.

Like you, I'm overwhelmed nearly every day by a steady barrage of need—suffering, injustice, despair, brokenness—all calling for more compassion than the world seems able to provide or any one of us can muster. How do we not become callous and numb or blindly indifferent? How do we engage meaningfully with the daily news, the hurts of our neighbors, and the stream of needs that confront us at every turn? How do we find hearts of compassion? How do we avoid hearts that may, like Dr. Seuss describes, be two sizes too small?

Compassion makes us human. In the face of what sometimes seems an uncaring world, we are part of a church that proclaims Christ's body present in each of us. We are part of a tradition that admonishes us to love our neighbor as our self. The compassionate body of Christ is unafraid to confront difficult issues of race and

gender, wealth and poverty, justice and peace. The compassionate body of Christ provides shelter for the homeless, food for the
hungry, money for the destitute, advocacy for the voiceless—recognizing that we, *all of us*, are broken, hungry, poor in spirit, and
in need of compassion.

Seeing the body of a little boy washed ashore from the cap-
sized boat his family used to escape the ravages of war in Syria or
the face of a young mother giving birth in a makeshift hospital in
a refugee camp in Eastern Europe is so wrenchingly painful that
we catch ourselves looking away. What will compassion mean if we
truly engage these images which are not just pictures on our television screens but real, living stories of unimaginable suffering?

What does it mean to have compassion? What does it mean
to be the body of Christ in the world? Can we truly enter into the
broken places, the shattered lives, the convoluted and complex political realities that make up our twenty-first-century world? How
do we see the world through the broken, loving heart of Christ?
Television commentators often warn us of images that may be
disturbing—"you may want to look away," they say. How, really, do
we love our neighbors as ourselves? Compassion surely will break
our hearts.

Teresa of Avila, a practical, no-nonsense sixteenth-century
saint and mystic, knew something about compassion:

> *Christ has no body on earth but yours.*
> *No hands but yours, no feet but yours.*
> *Yours are the eyes through which to look out*
> *Christ's compassion to the world.*
> *Yours are the feet with which he is to go about doing good.*
> *Yours are the hands with which he is to bless people now.*[1]

Compassion requires acts and deeds and yes, compassion
makes us human. Acts of compassion mean caring for one another
and those we'll never meet. Compassion is about political involve-
ment, willingness to embrace difficult issues, courage to expose
injustice and inequality, readiness and willingness to act. These are

---

1. Saint Teresa of Avila in her iconic poem, "Christ Has No Body."

acts of prayer, of entering into another's heart and hurt, another's suffering. These are acts of bravery, audacity, boldness, selflessness. Compassion exacts and demands commitment.

Compassion is feeding the hungry, clothing the naked, giving drink to the thirsty, visiting the imprisoned, caring for the sick, burying the dead, counseling the doubtful, instructing the ignorant, correcting sinners, comforting the sorrowful, forgiving all injuries, bearing wrongs with patience, praying for the living and the dead. These are the hard works of mercy, of compassion.

May we live uneasily with our comfortable and privileged lives. May we never grow heartless or insensitive. May our hearts be open to loosing the bonds of injustice, to undoing the thongs of the yoke, to letting the oppressed go free, to breaking every yoke (Isaiah 58:6). May our hearts be broken.

O God, help us to share your bread with the hungry, to bring the homeless poor into your house and ours, to acknowledge the naked and cover them, and not to hide ourselves from your own kin. Take away our hearts of stone. Make us your body, your hands, your feet. Make us your eyes for showing Christ's compassion to the world.

REFLECTION

If we truly allow ourselves the spirit of compassion—the *cost* of compassion—our worlds surely will be turned upside down. Our hearts will be broken. Compassion is more than concern, more than empathy, much more than understanding and kindness.

- In what ways does compassion entail more than concern or empathy, more than understanding and kindness?
- What does it mean to you that compassion is an act of prayer?
- How do we avoid having hearts of stone to become Christ's body, hands, feet?
- How do we become Christ's eyes for showing compassion to the world?
- What is the cost of compassion?

Devotion

Devotion

DEVOTION AS PRAYER? IT'S an odd word with multiple meanings. Its Latin root, *devitio*, means "total dedication." It also implies devotional acts—prayers and readings, rituals and practices—for focusing on God's presence. How might devotion become another lens for looking at the world—an attitude, a posture, another act of prayer?

This morning as I sit at our breakfast table, streams of warm sunshine spill across the room filling the open space with light and a tangible sense of well-being. In the tradition of Christians, I bow my head to offer a prayer of thanks for oatmeal and blueberries, for light and life and the day's work ahead of me. My Native American friends might dance or drum their devotion. Sufis would whirl their bodies in graceful circles of motion as their habit for expressing devotion. Buddhists likely would sit quietly. Hindus might offer sacrifices. Devote Jews probably would bob their heads back and forth. Showing devotion is to practice dedication and discipline. Devotion honors the gifts of life and makes holy the ordinary ground of ordinary lives. Devotion pulls us away from self-absorption and our ego-centered selves into the overwhelming love and amazing grace of God. The reverence of devotion makes space for the presence of the sacred.

Later in the morning, a dear friend and I spend an hour together catching up with each other's lives—a phone conversation, a holy discussion. We talk about things that matter and make a difference, issues that enrich our lives. We have known each other for almost fifty years; ours is a devoted friendship. As younger women, we spent hours together discussing thorny theological problems or wresting meaning out of the challenges of our particular stage in life. Now we are grandmothers who discover God's presence in the presence of one another.

In the afternoon, feeling guilty about the diversions that sometimes take me away from the discipline of writing, I glue myself to my computer and find there another experience of devotion. Writing becomes a devotional act marked by satisfaction and frustration, focus and fervor—"when it was good, it was very good and when it was bad, it was *really* bad." Writing becomes a holy deed, a thin place, prayer.

In between these ordinary events, there are exchanges of emails, a moment for watching the fog as it drapes itself across the mountains that preside over my corner of the world, time for working on a satisfying needlepoint project and imagining the next design waiting among my canvases, and the ever-present comfort of books, their siren call and mythic importance so much a part of my own holy ground.

As a child, my family made a habit of evening devotions. It was a way of centering ourselves and coming together to acknowledge our dependence and our need for God's presence in daily life. Later on when I was away at university, I would visit my grandparents who lived nearby. Rarely did I spend those occasional weekends with my grandparents that we didn't sit together around their kitchen table for devotions. Their profound faith was evident in the prayers they prayed for each of their grandchildren, for the hurts of the world, and for every other need they felt inclined to share. In their seemingly rock-solid belief in a God who was nearby, a God who took their everyday lives seriously, I learned something about devotion. And in those defining years of my own search for a God I could make sense of, their total dedication made a mark.

Living daily life as an act of devotion can expand our worldview, stretch our imaginations, inspire creativity. Even the ordinary tasks of daily life become extraordinary, worthy of worship and set apart. These experiences of devotion are thin places, described in

Celtic mythology as holy spaces where the visible and the invisible world come close, even touch. They are the holy ground of commitment and focus, dedication and perseverance.

Devotion makes more of us. It requires attention and single-mindedness. Devotion is life-giving, invigorating. The discipline of devotion draws us into the living presence of God and transforms our daily lives into prayer.

To what and to whom are you devoted? What is it that so captures your energy and your dedication that it makes more of you? What do you find worthy of dedication? How is devotion a holy act? And how do these acts of devotion shape for you a way of looking at the world, a way of praying? O God, give us the gift of devotion.

REFLECTION

Devotion makes more of us. It requires attention and single-mindedness. Devotion is life-giving, invigorating. It draws us into the living presence of God and transforms our daily lives into prayer.

- What is it that so captures your energy and your dedication that it makes more of you?
- Name some ways devotion moves us away from self-absorption into God's overwhelming love, God's amazing grace.
- How does living daily life as an act of devotion expand our worldview, stretch our imaginations, inspire creativity?

Enthusiasm

Enthusiasm

Nowhere is enthusiasm more evident than in the high-pitch fervor of athletic events. Whether one is an athlete, a sports enthusiast, or simply an observer, it is hard to think of athletic events—perhaps most especially the Olympic Games—without a spirit of enthusiasm. In addition to the faces that radiate unwavering hope, steely focus, energy and passion, there is an ever-present awareness of disciplined determination, talent, and years of demanding training that are standard requirements for athletes. No wonder enthusiasm is so central in sports.

But enthusiasm as prayer? "Really?" we say, perhaps feeling a bit put off. Maybe we're remembering stories of the Pentecostal movement where enthusiasm was kicked up a notch to give this denomination the derogatory moniker, "holy rollers." Or we may be picturing religious rallies or imagining other enthusiastic interpretations of Christian life and faith—television evangelists, religious hucksters selling their wares, or the zeal of someone whose life has been radically changed. "Really?" we say rather suspiciously.

We moderns tend to look down our noses at these expressions of enthusiasm—especially when it comes to religion. Religious groups have sometimes perpetrated horrific acts of violence in their zeal and unbridled passion. We rightly are wary and suspicious of extremes and unchecked fervor, especially in an era of fanaticism that stalks too many places in our world. Unless we're referring to a sporting event where enthusiasm is the name of the game, we try to avoid too much enthusiasm. We don't want to appear excessive, undignified, or childishly silly.

Yes—to all of this. But consider enthusiasm's multiple meanings: energetic interest, strong excitement, lively engagement, or my favorite: enthusiasm as "one with the energy of God." Enthusiasm is the quietly understated and dignified witness of French cook, Babette, in a classic Danish film, "Babette's Feast." To a staid and isolated Christian community who have eaten only fish broth and coarse bread all their lives, Babette serves a feast unlike any they have ever seen, much less tasted. In the pleasure of the food and the company around the table, Babette's quiet enthusiasm and passion for fine food results in an awakening of the senses, joy and pleasure, the burying of old grudges and rifts, and forgiveness and love.

Enthusiasm comes from planting seeds in dry and barren soil when, months later, those seeds have produced crops that will feed people around the world. It's what fuels commitments to justice-making and working for more peaceful neighborhoods and safer cities. It drives poets and musicians, artists and writers, teachers and robust leaders. It's the gift of hope and confidence, a declaration of the goodness of life and the generosity of God. Enthusiasm fuels optimism and courage.

The language of the church is hyperbole, a fancy word for overemphasizing, magnifying, or stating things with passion and enthusiasm. The Gospels are filled with stories meant to embody the overwhelming love of God in Christ. Many hymns of the church convey enthusiasm and the language of what homilist Fred Craddock calls "sacred excess." Trees clap. Rocks cry out. This universe we call home makes sense because of a loving, generative, compassionate God. How can we keep from singing! We stand on holy ground, at one with the energy of God. How can we not be enthusiastic!

The God who claims each of us is a God of abundance and excess, overflowing with unconditional love, grace upon grace, and generosity beyond our wildest imaginings. The God who claims and creates us in God's own image is the author, poet, painter, sculptor, and designer of a universe the scope and beauty of which escapes our comprehension. This same God creates and cares for the birds of the air and the lilies of the field. This same God walks with us in the darkest valleys, suffers with us, rejoices with us.

The spiritual quality of enthusiasm as prayer is tangible when we sing the liturgy, "Now the feast and celebration, all of creation sings for joy, to the God of life and love and freedom, praise and glory forever more!" or "This is the feast of victory for our God, Alleluia!"[1] We are singing our hearts out about a God of *life and love and freedom*—enthusiasm and exultation as prayer—joy that reverberates with the energy of God.

Babette wasn't able to stifle her enthusiasm for feasts. At great cost and even greater effort, she gathered together the elements of a fine meal: the best wines, delicately flavored soup, succulent cheeses and fine meats, fragrant breads and sweet dessert. The table was set with beautiful china and finest linen. There were candles, flowers, music. Then she called the dour community together, "Come, all is ready! Come, the feast is prepared!" Because of these things, she made a prayer of a meal. Because of these things, she was one with the energy of God. Because of this energy, she bore God to a pious, starving community on an isolated island along the Danish coast. May such energy and passion for life also be true of us!

REFLECTION

Consider enthusiasm's multiple meanings: energetic interest, strong excitement, lively engagement, or "one with the energy of God."

- What does it mean to you that the God who claims each of us is a God of abundance and excess, overflowing with unconditional love?
- Name some hymns or liturgies that best express enthusiasm as prayer.

1. Liturgies from *Evangelical Lutheran Worship*.

- How do you understand the spiritual quality of enthusiasm as prayer?
- Do you agree that the language of the church is hyperbole (a fancy word for overemphasizing, magnifying, stating things with passion and enthusiasm)? Why or why not?
- How is enthusiasm embodied in our understandings of God?

Faith

Faith

LISTEN! FAITH IS A way of life full of holes and questions. When I am filled with doubt and despair about never-ending cycles of injustice and suffering or when our self-satisfied and self-absorbed culture simply overwhelms our ability to cope or when I read of another shooting or massacre or bombing or experience the many ways we fail to care for the earth and our environment, it's easy to wonder where God is and how God works. Listen! Faith is hard.

All of us know ordinary and extraordinary people of faith. Often in quiet and unassuming ways, their lives speak God's presence in the midst of adversity and hardship. On occasion, their voices become sirens of passion calling us to act on behalf of others, pleading for justice, kindness, mercy—asking us to listen, calling us to be our best selves, calling us out of ourselves on behalf of others. Prayer is a way of being in the world and the act of faith, shaky as it may sometimes be, is what keeps us going much of the time.

Decade after decade, Palestinian prophet and pastor Dr. Mitri Raheb has worked with unrelenting determination to bring dignity and hope to the beleaguered people in the West Bank. His life, his work, his faith are one continuous prayer. In a recent book, *Faith in the Face of Empire*, Raheb writes a poignant history about oppression, tyranny, and living faithfully in a place where daily life and faith are under fire in ways unimaginable for most of us. The gift of this irrepressible faith has made it possible for Raheb to create places for hopefulness and steely determination. Without faith, he'd have given up long ago.

After the sorrow of 9–11, composer and writer Marty Haugen found himself in the depths of despair. I still can hear the wavering loneliness of Haugen's voice in a CD and book he wrote with Susan Briehl, *Turn My Heart: A Sacred Journey from Brokenness to Healing*:

> O God, why are you silent?
> I cannot hear your voice.
> The proud and strong and violent
> all claim you and rejoice.
> You promised you would hold me
> with tenderness and care.
> Draw near, O Love, enfold me,
> and ease the pain I bear.[1]

Mother Teresa, now named Saint Teresa of Calcutta, was a nun who devoted her life to the poor and knew the difficulty of faith. At the end of a long life devoted to caring for the broken, ignored, and despised—people cast off by the rest of society—she wrote about her own doubts and torments. Always humble to a fault, she'd spent a lifetime acting out the love of God. Her life embodied the love that is God. Pope Francis says of her, "She made her voice heard before the powers of this world so that they might recognize their guilt for the crime of poverty they created." Still, faith did not come easily for such a saint.

Listen! Our common longing for certitude of faith or some quantifiable way of defining God is tempting. When we are too weak or too filled with doubt or too full of ourselves, we depend on the faith of others—children, parents, and honest saints—whose lives also are marked by despair and doubt. We are carried by one another's prayers, born by one another's faith.

It's our task to remain human—to see the mystery of God in ordinary things and in ordinary people, even in ourselves. It's our task to pay attention, to immerse ourselves in the Psalms, where chapter after chapter recounts the human struggle to know God.

1. Briehl and Haugen, *Turn My Heart*, 4.

It's our task to put ourselves in places where we are fed and nourished and where we are sent into the world to make a difference for others. It's our task to embrace the world God continues to create, to see it as God's kingdom here and now, to help bring about God's reign of justice and peace in this place and time.

Listen! Faith is pure gift. It isn't an accomplishment or some definitive last word that means we finally understand the labyrinthine ways of the world or the quiet, unrelenting voice of the spirit of God at work amidst all the brokenness and all the suffering. It isn't self-assured contentment that God is in charge, a divine director on the set of a complicated movie. Faith is knowing what we do not know, yet trusting God to be that still small voice in every beating heart. Faith is rolling up our sleeves, getting to work, never giving up. Faith is hearing the breath of our neighbor and feeling the wounded spirit of a wounded world. Faith is prayer, holy ground. Listen to the God whose heart beats in each of our hearts, whose tears fall with our own, whose compassion knows no end— a God of love and grace and mercy.

O God, you have set us a banquet of love in the face of hatred, crowning us with love beyond our power to hold. Help us live faithfully. Help us to be bearers of faith and beacons of hope. Shepherd us, O God, beyond our wants, beyond our fears, from death into life!

REFLECTION

Prayer is a way of being in the world and the act of faith, shaky as it may sometimes be, is what keeps us going much of the time. Faith is hard.

- How is faith a way of life full of holes and questions?
- What does it mean to you that faith isn't an accomplishment or some definitive last word?
- Name a time you remember being carried by another's faith.

- Faith is knowing what we do not know, yet trusting God to be that still small voice in every beating heart. Does this ring true for you?

Gratitude

GRATITUDE

IT'S ONE OF THE first lessons parents teach their children. "What do you say?" we remind them, hoping they'll remember their manners when given a special gift or a compliment or any other act of generosity or thoughtfulness. "Thank you" is the hoped-for response, but more than the spoken words, we hope they will feel and express authentic appreciation. Gratitude as prayer is rooted in the knowledge that we are guests on this earth and recipients of its gifts, most of which come to us freely and without our asking. Gratitude is a lesson best learned early in life.

It also seems a natural expression of prayer, an attitude and a posture reflecting humility and appreciation—not shallow thanks but a deeply felt sense of gratefulness for life itself. Giving thanks both for the good that surrounds us as well as the challenges that try our souls should be as natural as breathing. But how do we summon authentic gratitude to God, how do we live thankfully without allowing it to become self-satisfied affirmation, God's special blessing in *my* life? How do we thank God when the world is in a bag of hurt?

These last months of horrific and senseless suffering—yet again in Europe and the United Kingdom, yet again in Israel and Palestine, yet again in Central America where children flee for their lives, yet again in the Ukraine and the U.S.—make me painfully aware that too many on our planet live in conditions where the *privilege of gratitude* is fleeting at best. How does one look at the images of traumatized children and decimated cities in war-torn Syria and not doubt a compassionate God?

Yes, I live uneasily with this sense of God's blessing and abundance. Yes, I know that my birth here rather than there makes all the difference. Does that mean that God has blessed me and not them? Why does the sun shine here and not there? How do we not twist gratitude into God's special blessing that at worst reeks of a God who favors some over others or a sense that God has blessed us in ways somehow withheld from others?

When we wake in the morning, grateful for the beauty of the world around us, eager to embrace meaningful work and aware that God is the giver of all life, how does our gratitude take into account the suffering all around us? What does gratitude mean when morning in so many places in the world is the beginning of another day of survival, hunger, darkness, and traumatizing fear?

In the title of a recent book by Anne Lamott, she describes what she sees as three essentials of prayer, *Help, Thanks, Wow.*[1] No stranger to suffering herself, Lamott is well acquainted with her own demons and struggles, and she is savvy about the darkness of the world. And so she begins with *help!* All of us know the place of fear from which that dreaded word comes, the pit in the bottom of our stomachs, the knowledge that we aren't in control, that we are vulnerable and in need of a God who walks with us when hopelessness or despair seem unbearable and overwhelming.

And then in the face of the absurdities of life, Lamott's next prayer is *thanks.* Not for having been singled out for specialness, not for having a corner on God's blessing, but in simple gratitude that God is God, that God lives *with* us in the darkness and the fear—in the bombings and shootings and in endless cycles of oppression and injustice. To be able to live with gratitude in those places where hope is elusive and God's presence only a dim glimmer on the horizon requires so much more than a simple attitude of thanksgiving.

Gratitude is a way of life, a way of being. It's a lens through which we see and acknowledge God's presence within us, God's

1. Lamott, *Help, Thanks, Wow.*

very life in ours, and God's desire for wholeness and unity—truly holy ground. Even in the wrenching challenges of life, those who live with gratitude appreciate and give thanks for a new day, for companionship, for things paltry and things significant because they know that our very breath is a gift and our lives, however broken or challenging, are sacred dwelling places for the Holy One.

Lamott is honest enough to know that God's presence within and without is mystery and that none of us understands how this works. She knows that life isn't fair. But she celebrates God's presence nonetheless because she knows God to be the Holy One, the crucified Christ who also knows sorrow and grief and fear. Gratitude is a way of life, a way of being. It's a lens through which we see and acknowledge God's presence within us, God's very life in ours. Help, thanks, and yes, wow!

REFLECTION

Gratitude is a way of life, a way of being. It's a lens through which we see and acknowledge God's presence within us, God's very life in ours, and God's desire for wholeness and unity—truly holy ground.

- How do we summon authentic gratitude to God, how do we live gratitude without allowing it to become self-satisfied affirmation, God's special blessing in *my* life?
- In what ways might gratitude be a privilege?
- How do we thank God when the world is in a bag of hurt?
- What does it mean to you that God in Christ knows sorrow, grief? Why does it matter?
- How does gratitude become a way of life, authentic grace, prayer?

Hospitality

Hospitality

IN A CLASSIC BOOK about experiencing the sacred in daily life (*Spiritual Literacy: Reading the Sacred in Everyday Life*), authors Frederic and Mary Ann Brussat define hospitality as a practice, a way of welcoming guests as well as new and alien ideas with graciousness. How might gracious welcome—both of people and ideas—become prayer, a way for recognizing the living presence of God and a way of welcoming Christ?

For almost as long as I can remember, creating warm and welcoming spaces for gathering has been a basic instinct, a passion. As children, we cobbled together beach houses in the sand using driftwood to mark the rooms where we would welcome siblings and cousins. We made wide entrances and opened "the doors" to meeting places and eating places. We brought bread sacks filled with sandwiches and found shelter there among the driftwood, safe above the rising tide.

Our homes, a log cabin on a beautiful island and parsonages where people expected to be welcomed with regularity, became hubs for family gatherings and comfortable spaces for gathering with others. My grandparents' sprawling and hospitable house was another gathering place, a home where friends and relatives came together to share gossip, argue and debate, feast on one another's best recipes, and catch up on each other's lives. Around picnic tables and dining tables and coffee tables, lively topics like religion and politics were discussed and deliberated, subjects we knew might not curry favor but would keep everyone sitting on the edges of their seats.

Later, my desire to share hospitality came in the form of dorm rooms, first apartments, spaces where afternoon tea could be shared, and university flats where simple dinners were occasions for sharing good food and stimulating conversation—all of them sheltering spaces, holy ground, safe, protected, sacred. In many of those places, there were new people to meet and get to know, new connections with families different from my own, sometimes even cultural and religious differences to be probed and understood, all venues ripe for learning.

Hospitality begins with curiosity and eagerness to embrace and be interested in others. It's about sharing who we are and what we have. In a world where strangers often are feared and where all of us are guilty of shunning "the other", hospitality requires risk. It asks us to trust, to open ourselves, to show generosity and genuine interest in others. Joan Chittister describes it as the way we come *out of ourselves.* Perhaps that is one of the ways hospitality becomes prayer.

On occasion, our places of hospitality become forts meant to keep others out. Rather than opening doors and minds, rather than coming *out of ourselves,* we try to protect ourselves by building fences or walls and shoring up our prejudices and tightly held convictions. We lock the doors and bar the windows out of fear and vulnerability. It's so much easier for us to show hospitality to those with whom we agree, to those who are "our people", to those who share our worldviews. Too often when we invite people into our own home, I am painfully aware of how consistently we choose people we know or find interesting or with whom we feel a certain kinship. Welcoming strangers—especially those on the fringes of society, especially those who see the world differently—is hard.

When we were very young, my mother told us that a woman we did not know but who occasionally brought fruit to our door might be an angel. Of course, we were transfixed by the thought. It was my mother's version of welcoming strangers, showing hospitality, entertaining angels and thus welcoming Christ.

Hospitality as prayer makes space for honesty and intimacy. One feels its embrace because it is interested in and accepting of others. True hospitality welcomes new ideas by showing genuine tolerance and curiosity, even compassion. In those spaces of hospitality, God is present and God's grace is tangible. There is largesse of spirit and palpable generosity.

The Psalmist tells of a God who prepares a table of welcome where guests are protected from the attack of enemies—"You prepare a table before me in the presence of my enemies." Perhaps the writer is speaking of more than a safe place, affirming both acceptance and safety. May we show such hospitality. May it be a way of praying for us where we come out of ourselves to open our doors and welcome strangers, a holy place where we see Christ in one another. O God, make us willing to share the wonder and the frustration of being human. Make each of our corners of the world, of the universe, sheltering places where friends and family—even strangers and perhaps enemies—can find rest and peace, grace and acceptance.

REFLECTION

Hospitality is a practice, a way of welcoming guests as well as new and alien ideas with graciousness, a way of welcoming Christ.

- What does it mean to you that hospitality begins with curiosity and an eagerness to embrace and be interested in others?
- How does hospitality require risk? Why is it so hard?
- What might the Psalmist mean telling us of a God who prepares a table of welcome where guests are protected from the attack of enemies—"You prepare a table before me in the presence of my enemies"?
- How does hospitality as prayer make space for honesty and intimacy?
- Do you agree with Joan Chittister that hospitality is the way we *come out of ourselves*? Why or why not?

Imagination

Imagination

USING ONE'S IMAGINATION WAS easy when, as children in the un-inhibited abandon of summertime, we could sleep outside beneath an immense panoply of the heavens. Among my earliest memories of summer on the island where I grew up is gathering old and musty sleeping bags in the late afternoon to lay them out in a sheltered place among the logs and driftwood where we'd be protected from the tide. In anticipation of our nighttime adventure, we'd clear a space in the soft sand so that when darkness finally came, we'd be ready.

Filled with awe and expectation and no small amount of wonder, we watched for blinking satellites and falling stars. Prayer and imagination went hand in hand. And as we pulled blankets up over our ears to stifle the night sounds of owls and a sense of the insignificance of ourselves and our small island world, prayer and imagination were of a piece. "Now I lay me down to sleep. I pray dear Lord my soul to keep." The sense of the infinite was palpable, begging for curiosity and imagination.

Childhood itself can be a wellspring of imagination. Without the complexities of life experience or the weight of too many explanations, children explore and dream with abandon. They aren't hampered by reason and there is always something new to be touched, smelled, discovered, contemplated. The possibilities are infinite.

When we "grow up", it is sometimes harder for us to put ourselves in places where awe and wonder fuel imagination and fire our ability to explore the world. As adults, perhaps imagination becomes a creative way for changing our circumstances or contributing to making the world a better place. Visionaries must be imaginative. Prophets must see what others ignore. Dreamers help us imagine a better world.

Imagination invites creativity and engagement with wonder. Growing up on an island—a place set apart, a magical place—allowed us nonstop opportunities for exploring the mysteries, things we could not explain, seen and unseen. In the quiet beauty of that place, in the silence and simple ways of children, there was space for encountering God.

The astonishing spectacle of that night sky in a place where light pollution was almost non-existent is forever etched in my being. It became a permanent backdrop for my imagination, an ever-expanding canvas for considering God's creative and mysterious presence and the wonder of our own existence. The seeming deep silence of the galaxies above us, the steady movement of the tide and the rhythm of waves lapping against the shore, and the night sounds of elusive nocturnal creatures became part of the drama, leaving us speechless and awe-struck.

To this day, the imagination sparked by the majesty of a universe so beyond our grasp best captures for me the meaning of prayer—simply standing in silence and humility before the handiwork of the Creator. We need no words and certainly no formulaic prayers for speaking to God or listening for God. It is enough to join in the wonder of being human: integral to the vast workings of the universe and knowing ourselves to be part of the inscrutable ways of the sacred. Is this a tiny glimpse of the God who lives within each of us? Is this a taste of what it means to be created in the image of God?

Those night sounds—the hooting of owls, the rustle of leaves, and perhaps the scurrying of small animals in the woods behind us—were also part of imagination as prayer. God, are you here with us? It's easy to picture you holding forth out there in the vastness of space, but here among the fears of the night, are you here too? And in the warmth of our musty sleeping bags, we pulled our pillows closer waiting for sleep to come.

In the morning, our beachside beds now damp with dew, the world was a whole different place. The tide had gone out leaving a long expanse of exposed beach. Once we'd fully wakened, we'd dress and eat and then accompanied by the cries of seagulls circling above, we'd explore the tidelands where crabs and starfish and sand dollars lay exposed to the warm morning sun. Imagination? The place was a feast for every one of the senses. And even as a young child, I knew God's presence here.

O God, help us reclaim our childlike imaginations. Show us your face in the ordinary stuff of life. Make us comfortable speaking to you in silence. Help us hear your voice in the sounds of nature and in the wonder of the universe that surrounds us. Most of all, help us imagine the world as you intend it to be: holy ground, an earthly Eden, a fruitful garden, a place of justice and peace, and a sanctuary for us and all your creatures.

REFLECTION

To this day, the imagination sparked by the majesty of a universe so beyond our grasp best captures for me the meaning of prayer—simply standing in silence and humility before the handiwork of the Creator.

- Where and when do you feel a palpable sense of the infinite?
- Visionaries must be imaginative. Prophets must see what others ignore. Dreamers help us imagine a better world. Who are some visionaries/prophets/dreamers for you?
- What are some ways we might reclaim our childhood—and perhaps childlike—imaginations?
- Where do you make space for encountering God?

Joy

JOY

I TREASURE A SIMPLE story shared by anthropologist Loren Eiseley as one poignant picture of joy.[1] It hardly compares to so many images of human elation—homecomings, births, happy endings to dire predictions—but its raw meaning more than conveys the essence of joy. Eiseley tells of capturing a small hawk in the dark rafters of an old barn. He was doing work for a zoo and had been hoping for just such a fine specimen. In spite of a ferocious fight, Eiseley finally had the little hawk in his bleeding hands, but the hawk's mate, who had been directly in the throes of the melee, escaped. Eiseley was relieved—he wasn't sure he'd have been able to handle both of them and it was clear that the male hawk had saved his mate by diverting attention to himself.

After some time, the small hawk gave up the fight and Eiseley laid his limp body in a cage planning later to retrieve him. Returning the next morning, he looked up at the sky one more time thinking he might see the female, but she seemed to be gone for good. So he gently took the now nearly lifeless body of the captured hawk in his hands and whether consciously or not, laid him on the ground. The hawk lay there for a minute or more without moving, his clouded eyes gazing toward the vault of sky above them. Suddenly as if he'd been reborn, the male hawk was gone, soaring away and out of sight straight into the blinding rays of the sun.

Then Eiseley describes hearing a piercing sound of joy— "unutterable and ecstatic joy"—that came ringing down from the

1. Eiseley, "A Cry of Joy."

mountain peaks high above him. The hawk was soaring straight into the sun and Eiseley could now see his mate further up where she likely had been waiting for him since the capture the day before. That ineffable and indescribable cry of joy etched itself into Eiseley's being. And for me, his telling of the story captures not only the joy he felt as a scientist releasing what was meant to be wild but also the elation of the two hawks whose cries were the very essence of joy.

Joy comes from a place deep within us. It isn't about happiness or contentment or a fleeting sense of well-being. It isn't sentimental nor does it ignore the common realities of worry, fear, grief, hardships. It's much more than a veneer that wears thin with time. Joy is the essence of the nature of God. Joy is not one of the components of Christianity, said Orthodox priest Alexander Schmemann; it is the tonality—the sound, pitch, timbre, tone— that penetrates *everything*. It comes from deep within us where even in the darkest of times, we know that God dwells with us and in us. Joy itself is prayer.

It would be silly, certainly unproductive, and probably unhealthy to ignore the many ways joy eludes us. None of us is exempt from sorrow and hardship and it takes only a cursory look at the nightly news and the daily vicissitudes of ordinary life to know the sadness of the world. And of course it would be wrong (not to mention impossible) for us to turn our backs on suffering or ignore everyday regrets so that, in spite of it all, we might be joyful.

We all know people who radiate a quiet kind of joy. I don't mean an off-putting corner on happiness that somehow precedes them wherever they go like some cloying perfume. I mean people whose lives may be riddled with difficult challenges and yet they seem to draw from a deep well of contentment and peace. They are able to see God's face and to hear God's voice in the clamor of life. Without being superficial, they find authentic joy in the good and the bad, in justice and injustice, in things gained and things lost. Jewish theologian Martin Buber called this holy joy the beating heart of the universe.

At the heart of joy is the heart of God. A painting by John August Swanson called *Festival of Lights* (1991) illustrates, for me, joy as prayer. Across the green, rolling hills that stretch into the background of his colorful work come streams of people, their myriad faces turned heavenward shining in the light of the candles they carry and the starry night above them. This is the joy of the feast of the Nativity, the joy of a God who takes human form becoming incarnate, one of us. It's the joy of the feast of the Resurrection, an Eastering God who brings life out of death, hope out of despair. It's the joy of a God who makes all things new.

Joy is life-giving and infectious. Like the God who is its source, it shines beyond itself to illumine the beauty and goodness of life. Across an ever-expanding universe and in the minutest details of our lives, God's presence is the sound, the pitch, the timbre, and the tone of holy joy. *Now the feast and celebration, all of creation sings for joy—to the God of life and love and freedom, praise and glory forever more!* This prayer of joy reverberates with the goodness of God and life together: *God has come to dwell with us, to make us people of God; to make all things new!* May the God of life and love and freedom bring you joy!

REFLECTION

Joy is not one of the components of Christianity, said Orthodox priest Alexander Schmemann; it is the tonality—the sound, pitch, timbre, tone—that penetrates *everything*. It comes from deep within us where even in the darkest of times, we know that God dwells with us and in us.

- Who do you know who sometimes radiates a sense of authentic joy?
- What does it mean to you that at the heart of joy is the heart of God?
- Do you agree that joy is the essence of the nature of God? Why or why not?
- When have you felt life-giving, infectious joy?
- How might joy itself be prayer?

Kindness

KINÐNESS

I WILL NEVER FORGET a bus trip one summer day, riding a packed-full red double-decker up Banbury Road to our tiny little flat north of Summertown. We'd lived in Oxford a full year by then and I was lonesome for home and carrying a heavy load of groceries in my stuffed canvas bags, on my way to fetch our two young daughters at the close of the school day. As I found the only vacant seat on that crowded bus, I noticed an elderly woman sitting in the seat just behind me. She was small and frail looking and in her lap she balanced two small cartons of strawberries. As I sat down, she suddenly tapped me on the shoulder and handed me one of the cartons, clearly offering a gift, clearly showing extraordinary kindness. She was a stranger but I took it, thanked her profusely, and got off at my stop with a lighter step, a sense of gratitude, and a memory of unexpected kindness. It wasn't the first time I'd been a recipient of such unanticipated generosity but I've never forgotten that moment of kindness. Those years in England were marked by such acts.

As I write this day, it is my birthday and I've spent the afternoon reading more than a hundred birthday notes—little visits from friends and family who kindly have remembered the day of my birth. It's one of the benefits of social media: up pops the name of someone you know reminding you of their birthday and you send a quick note, a warm wish. And today before the day had barely begun, I was serenaded by a birthday polka, a bouquet of balloons, a picture of a newly sprouted amaryllis bulb, and many warm wishes. Such kindness. Such generosity.

Kindness as prayer, a spiritual practice? Absolutely! All of us can recall special acts of kindness, a word, a welcome, a touch that conveys generosity and largesse. The word kindness itself comes from a Latin root, *genere*. It means "to beget." Kindness is about generativity, begetting. It makes more of us and it makes more of others. Kindness begets life. It is life-giving and life-enriching, a spiritual practice and an act of affirmation. Kindness bestows grace and care and love. And it's another of the definitions of prayer.

When we were growing up and somehow began criticizing or unfairly analyzing someone's behavior or attitude—something we did more often than I like to admit as a way of affirming our own fragile corner on great wisdom or shrewd psychological insight— my father often would say, "Be kind, be kind. You never know what battles another person may be fighting." For all of us who too easily make judgments or too quickly are negative, whose default is to criticize, a word of grace is in order. We are the undeserving recipients of God's extraordinary grace. We are heirs—inheritors—of resurrection life, the freeing good news of God's love, forgiveness, generosity, generativity. We are made in God's image. We bear Christ to one another and we bear God's resurrecting power to the world. We are the begetters of kindness.

And yet, it goes without saying that Christians don't have a corner on kindness. It takes only a moment to remember sordid stories of oppression and Christianity's history of violent wars and persecutions. If we're honest, we also know that the church often is torn apart by petty disagreements, voracious gossip, cultures of criticism. None of us can claim kindness as our primary lens for seeing our neighbors or the larger world around us. The little song, "They Will Know We Are Christians by Our Love" has always felt a bit too smug, perhaps even outright self-righteous, and too often self-deceiving.

With each birthday note today, I am reminded of a relationship important to my life. I picture faces and shared experiences. I hear the sounds of their voices and delight in their affection, a literal shower of prayers of love and kindheartedness, truly kindness as prayer.

God's lavish love and mercy are the heart of what it means to be human. We are called to embody Christ's sacrificial life, to be Christ to one another and to the hurting world we inhabit. Practicing kindness as a way of life is to share and *to be* God's extravagant love and mercy. May our lives shine with the luminosity of kindness, not for the sake of kindness itself, though that is worthy too, but because we reflect the overwhelming love of Christ.

REFLECTION

Kindness is about generativity, begetting. It makes more of us and it makes more of others. Kindness begets life. It is life-giving and life-enriching, a spiritual practice and an act of affirmation. Kindness bestows grace and care and love.

- Name a time when you were the recipient of extraordinary kindness. Describe how you felt.
- Can you recall showing generous kindness yourself? What was the occasion?
- How does kindness beget life? Become prayer?
- How is practicing kindness a way of *being* God's extravagant love and mercy?

LISTENING

Listening

"Hear 'dat?" he says with wonder in his voice and again, "hear 'dat?" My little grandson, no matter how absorbed he may be in something else, no matter how busy or wound up, always stops in his tracks at the sound of the train whistling by our little village in Glacier National Park. Elliot's ability to hear the whistling train makes us stop to listen as well. He's enthralled by trains and the magic of winding through the mountains, in and out of tunnels, across high bridges, around narrow, meandering river valleys, rumbling and roaring into the distance. Elliot's ability to imagine where the train has come from and where it might be going comes from listening.

Be still, listen, and know that I am God. From life in the womb punctuated by the steady beating of our mother's heart and the swoosh of amniotic fluid around us all the way to the very end of our days, when hearing often is among the last of our faculties, we are surrounded by sound. Sometimes it's deafening and we want to block it out. Sometimes we listen with every fiber in our being because it's subtle, elusive. Much of the time, we listen without being aware of listening.

Be still, listen, and know that I am God. Scientists remind us that the universe is an amazing symphony of sound pulsating with music and rhythm. For me there is nothing quite so compelling as the rhythmic music of waves against the beach, the shrill cry of seagulls, the steady patter of rain. God's presence is almost always tangible in those experiences.

But a good share of the time, listening seems to elude us. Perhaps it is age: there's so much we want to say about life and time is running out. And the older we get it seems, the more we have to say. Too often we love the sound of our own voices, the wisdom of our years, a perceived notion that our vast understanding of life should be shared—at length. Too often when someone is talking to us, we allow our minds to wander or race to what *we* might say next rather than truly listening and hearing the other. Too often, we ignore the sounds around us. Listening is an art. It requires cultivation.

Be still, listen, and know that I am God. Hearing one another to speech is a gift.[1] Hearing one another to speech honors the other by valuing their voice, their opinions, their feelings. Making space to listen, giving another an opportunity to speak while providing ears to receive is an affirmation, a validation. It requires me to put away my own need for being heard and my own version of wait, wait, I have something important to say! It's a way of listening another's soul into being, a way of prayer.

"Listen to your life," Frederick Buechner reminds us. "See your life for the fathomless mystery it is." Rather than endless talking *to* God, we might do well to quiet ourselves and consider listening to God in all the sounds within and around us. I remember listening to my grandfather recite poetry. He also loved to sing rhymes and tell stories and I delighted in his pleasure as much as I enjoyed the words themselves. Sometimes when I recall the sounds of my parents' or grandparents' voices, I visualize their presence and all the ways they shared life and faith and the conundrums of being family. I am grateful for a long line of ancestors who told stories of faith, who with all their idiosyncrasies and human limitations

---

1. Hearing one another to speech is a feminist expression I came upon many years ago. Theologian Nelle Morton first used this phrase in an essay in 1977 called "Beloved Image." Later she developed the idea about empowering one another by hearing the other to speech in her book, *The Journey Is Home*. She and Elaine Pagels elaborated on this theme—women literally hearing one another to speech—at the 1971 Conference on Women. Nelle Morton (1905–87) was a church activist for racial justice, a teacher, and a leading voice in the movement for women's spirituality and feminist theology.

surrounded us with love and grace. In listening to them, I learned to hear God's beating heart within my own beating heart within the beating heart of the world—as a form of prayer.

When our grandchildren come to visit, I often tuck them in at night in their beds under the low eave of their upstairs bedroom. I remind them to listen: "Shhh, do you hear the rain splashing on the roof above your head? Listen! Can you hear the river rushing by outside the window? God gives us rain to make things grow. The river is God's gift, a place to swim, to fish, to play. Shhh."

Be still, listen, and know that I am God.

REFLECTION

From life in the womb punctuated by the steady beating of our mother's heart and the swoosh of amniotic fluid around us all the way to the very end of our days, when hearing often is among the last of our faculties, we are surrounded by sound. *Be still, listen, and know that I am God.*

- "Listen to your life," Frederick Buechner reminds us. How do you do this?
- What sounds or experiences of listening best convey God's presence for you?
- Too often, we ignore the sounds around us. Listening is an art. It requires cultivation. How do you cultivate the art of listening?
- What does it mean to be still, listen, and know that God is present? That God is?
- How is this prayer?

Mindfulness

Mindfulness

Hileama and Sarra were Muslim friends of mine. We lived together in a block of university flats where our rituals and habits were part of the daily routine. We'd often share a cup of tea late in the day, watching our little ones play, savoring conversation, delighting in learning from one another. Their worlds were so different from mine. I wanted to know more about growing up in an Islamic African culture; they were curious about "religious" Americans and what it meant to be a Pro-tes-tant, which gave me pause and helped clarify my own understandings of the Protestant Reformation. But in the waning light of wintery afternoons, Hileama and Sarra would stop mid-sentence, gather their children, and hurry back to their tiny flats where prayer mats lay open on cold, tiled floors waiting for bent knees, afternoon prayers, mindful attention.

Mindfulness as prayer? Multi-tasking is the name of the game I know best. I seem to measure the days by how many tasks I've accomplished, what projects have been tended to, what new things I might find interesting and fulfilling. It isn't that I *have* to be busy; it's that I *love* to be busy. It's a measure of my identity, productivity, my worth. Life is short after all and one does not want to waste time, linger, or dilly dally for goodness sake. And so I make lists, legendary lists—long categories of things to do, places to go, people I want to see, emblematic *perhaps* of a full and rich life. But maybe, just maybe, my voluminous lists should include, "Stop! Pay attention! Listen! Be!"

In childhood, we'd spend hours dallying in rowboats along the beach looking for bottom fish or scurrying crabs. We'd build forts up above the tideline among the logs and driftwood, staking out rooms and decorating them with twigs and wild flowers. At night under the dark sky we'd watch for the movement of blinking satellites and falling stars, always in awe of God's creation. What happened along the way to adulthood? Where do we get the notion that to be productive there must be non-stop activity? Or that our worth depends on a schedule or a list or a set of accomplishments?

Practicing mindfulness is not easy. Our tradition doesn't require us to lay out prayer mats or stop the clock for attentive prayer. Our culture encourages us to focus on ourselves, our own self-interests. To stop honestly, to screen out all the noise of our busy lives, to quiet ourselves long enough to pay attention seems too often out of reach. Has adulthood robbed us of the ability to live mindfully?

In her most recent book, *Learning to Walk in the Dark,* author Barbara Brown Taylor describes her amazement at the idea of differentiating between trees by the sounds of their shadows. This amazing ability to listen so carefully, so mindfully, to the *sounds of shadows* is the gift of one who, having completely lost the sight of his eyes as a young person, also describes seeing: "I could not see the light of the world anymore. Yet the light was still there. I had only to receive it."[1]

It's disconcerting to think that we who have "eyes to see and ears to hear" may not see or hear very well at all. We do not know how to be still, how to see beneath the surface of things, how to hear the sounds of tree shadows. We do not know how to quiet ourselves or how to stop the interminable voices running through our minds and in our heads.

Practicing mindfulness is a lifelong challenge. Slowing down long enough to notice an early morning moon as it tilts away into the western sky is an act of mindfulness. Taking time to listen to one another, to notice and sense another's joy or worry, to be

1. Taylor, *Learning to Walk,* 103.

present simply with silence is a sacred act of prayer. Stopping long enough to be attentive makes us more alive.

God rests on our eyelids, says Jewish rabbi Abraham Joshua Heschel, but we are too busy to notice. Heschel also reminds us that just to be is a blessing and just to live is holy. May we learn to dally again, to linger and stop mid-sentence and mid-task. May we take time to be mindful, to see beneath the surface of things, behind our eyelids, where God rests and waits for us to notice.

REFLECTION

Mindfulness as prayer? Multi-tasking is the name of the game I know best. I seem to measure the days by how many tasks I've accomplished, what projects have been tended to, what new things I might find interesting and fulfilling. It isn't that I *have* to be busy; it's that I *love* to be busy.

- Rabbi Abraham Joshua Heschel reminds us that just to be is a blessing, just to live is holy. What might this mean for you?
- How does mindfulness make us more alive? More receptive to God's presence, God's spirit?
- How do you practice presence? How might simple silence become a sacred act of prayer?
- Where are some places and what are some ways for getting away from our frenetic culture and life-styles to be truly mindful?

Nurturing

Nurturing

How do we think about who and what God is or what the spirit of God is like? Many of us wrestle with the notion of "God out there," a tiered understanding of the universe replete with a God who lives "up" in heaven while we work things out "down" here on earth. It was the conventional way of describing the cosmos, the way the ancients interpreted mystery—God as the creator, a divine male image, reigning as a king or ruler overseeing the affairs of the world, a monarch—found often in the language of the Old Testament. It's not easy to replace Sunday school notions or mythological understandings of a hierarchical God who rules the universe with might and power.

In this twenty-first century, many of us are looking for new ways to think about who and what God is, knowing full well that the God we seek to define is beyond language and pictures. And yet, we moderns like to think we've come a long way as interpreters of wisdom. Sometimes we're even a bit puffed up about life-changing advancements in medicine, science, technology. But in the realm of spiritual life, I want to go back a few centuries.

Mechtild of Magdeburg was a thirteenth-century mystic. Like many mystics, Mechtild pushed the boundaries of confining definitions of God. She lived in medieval times and yet she understood God as a nurturing mother. Like many other saints and mystics, she was bold about exploring new ways for understanding God and her image of God as a nurturing mother is yet another description of prayer.

I am a mother of three daughters. Recalling each of their births, the sense of awe and unabashed wonder about their "being" was completely overwhelming, even incomprehensible. God as creator giving me the gift of creation is a powerful experience of generativity. Those searing moments of pushing a living child out of my body are etched forever in my psyche. They are perhaps the closest I will come to knowing the presence and mystery of God who creates and makes of us creators.

These beautiful daughters of mine now have little ones of their own. I watch each of them care for their children with the same devotion and nurturing presence that was lavished on them. The image of God as nurturing mother fills me with an overpowering sense of gratitude. In my own longing to find words and images for a God who creates life, who takes our form, who nurtures us, there is deep joy and affirmation in imagining God as a mother. "Mothering God, you gave me birth; . . . mothering Christ, you took my form; . . . mothering Spirit, nurturing one . . ."[1]

The image of God birthing the world—the universe—as a nurturing mother is fitting. It helps us understand God as the source of all life and it shows us the wonder of creation and of creating. This nurturing aspect of "God-ness" helps us know ourselves to be made in God's image. It profoundly enriches our sense of who we are and it affirms the sacredness of our lives. It's a way of communing with God, a way of praying, and yet another lens for seeing God in our midst.

How can we help one another embrace this God in our very midst? And how is the mystery of a nurturing God conveyed in metaphors that nourish and sustain us even as we struggle to understand ourselves as God's home? When God is no longer "out there"—some sort of divine monarch ruling over us—but *here*, here in this place, the holy ground of this earth home, we can begin to know God as a nurturing mother, loving father, eternal spirit, earth-maker, pain-bearer, life-giver, the source of all that is and that shall be. When God's home is here, when our lives are the roads God travels and God's kingdom is the holy ground of

1. Text based on the writings of Julian of Norwich.

this earth home, we begin to experience God as the very breath of life, a nurturing God whose spirit of love and unconditional mercy lives within us.

Words and images for God always will be limited, inadequate, partial. But I find deep comfort in Mechtild of Magdeburg's thirteenth-century interpretation. Her prophetic and courageous description of God as a nurturing mother does indeed push the boundaries of confining definitions of God. She *was* bold and the prophet Isaiah's description is a strikingly graphic echo:

> . . . *that you may nurse and be satisfied from her consoling breast; that you may drink deeply with delight from her glorious bosom . . . and you shall nurse and be carried on her arm, and dandled on her knees. As a mother comforts her child, so I will comfort you.*

—Isaiah 66:11, 12b, 13a

Prayer indeed!

REFLECTION

The image of God birthing the world—the universe—as a nurturing mother is fitting. It helps us understand God as the source of all life and it shows us the wonder of creation and of creating. This nurturing aspect of "God-ness" helps us know ourselves to be made in God's image. It profoundly enriches our sense of who we are and it affirms the sacredness of our lives. It's a way of communing with God, a way of praying, and yet another lens for seeing God in our midst.

- Describe some of the ways you think about who and what God is, what the spirit of God is like.
- In what ways does the nurturing aspect of "God-ness" help us know ourselves to be made in God's image? Why or why not is this difficult for us?
- Words and images matter. Think about the words and images for God that you use. If they are primarily male images and male adjectives, why?

- What do the words of Mechtild of Magdeburg's thirteenth-century interpretation—God as a nurturing mother—mean for you?
- How might the words from Isaiah 66—*As a mother comforts her child, so I will comfort you*—function as prayer?

Openness

Openness

A PRIZED MEMORY FROM my childhood is an occasion my mother called "open house." For her they often were part of a dreaded expectation: hosting people in a way she imagined to be part of her responsibility as the spouse of a pastor, a sense of duty trumping her ever-present anxieties. Open houses occurred mostly at Christmas when our home finally was bedecked in Christmas regalia and endless tins of bars and cookies, krumkakke, jule kage, and pickled herring had been stashed away in preparation for the big day.

As an extroverted daughter in this family of mine, I loved all the hoop-la and couldn't wait for the hoards to begin arriving. Later in my life, those open houses became the template for open houses of our own: frequent faculty gatherings, baptismal celebrations, confirmations, graduations. I associate all of them with an expansive sense of welcome, friends and neighbors coming and going, great food, music and laughter, and the voices of people savoring one another's company.

These experiences of open house are memorable for me in part because they point to a sense of openness. Open house meant inviting more than family and more than friends. I understood it to mean wide-open doors, fresh air, a way of welcoming old and new friends and people we didn't know well. And even though it evoked dread in my mother—endless cleaning, baking, and fussing—for me it was an opportunity for a welcoming party I didn't want to miss.

Holding open house in our hearts is to practice openness. Openness is a spiritual practice, a way of praying, requiring us to listen and to be present, accepting others as well as ourselves. Openness may mean that others see all the shortcomings, all the blemishes and flaws that characterize every one of us. We may be critiqued for one thing or another and our open houses may not measure up to the expectations of others or even ourselves. These are the dreaded risks.

Openness can sometimes be interpreted as naïve. When we jump into the fray of refugee resettlement and all its complexities or when we voice our opinions and hard-fought convictions about issues of justice or care of our earth home or when we stand with people whom society may see as risky or dangerous or speak on behalf of neighbors or strangers whose rights are being violated, we open ourselves to judgment, even ridicule for lacking common sense or savviness about the "real world." Sometimes these words can be euphemisms for ignoring the troubles all around us. When we close our eyes and our hearts to the deep hurt of the world, we are complicit in all the downward spirals of death. We close our doors and forget at our risk that we are indeed our neighbors' keeper, earth keepers, peace keepers—key actors for opening hearts and minds to making the world a better place.

But when we practice openness and learning how to love, we make visible our own humanity. It's what we are called to do and to be—a way of life, a way of prayer. When we practice openness, we show others acceptance and generosity of spirit allowing them to be themselves. When we open the doors of our own lives, we make ourselves vulnerable to others.

Openness as prayer is an attitude and a condition of acceptance most of us struggle with throughout life. We're much more inclined to analyze and criticize. We like placing ourselves in positions of judgment where we can cast our opinions far and wide. To hold open house in our hearts for all people and all things means space for experiencing our shared humanity, space for God to speak and act, space for openness and acceptance. To hold open house in our hearts is a metaphor for carrying one another and bearing the joys and sorrows of life together.

Open your doors, open your hearts, fling wide the windows of your soul! Make space for yourself that embraces the warts and foibles we all share. Make space for everyone you meet, welcoming them to your open house, allowing them a place of acceptance and affirmation. Make space for God to speak and act, to inhabit your life. Holding open house in our hearts is a risk worth taking. Openness is a spiritual practice that can change the world!

REFLECTION

Holding open house in our hearts is a metaphor for carrying one another and bearing the joys and sorrows of life together. Openness is a spiritual practice, a way of praying, requiring us to listen and to be present, accepting others as well as ourselves.

- What keeps us from opening our doors, our hearts?

- When we open the doors of our own lives, we make ourselves vulnerable to others. Name some ways practicing openness shows others acceptance and generosity of spirit and allows them to be themselves.

- How might open house in our hearts make space for God to speak and act?

- How is practicing openness a way of life, a way of prayer?

P LAY

Play

As I REFLECT ON play as a spiritual practice, it is summer now and our family home in Glacier Park is filled with children and grand-children. Arriving as they do with bicycles and paddle boards and hiking gear, we welcome them with other surprises: water toys and butterfly nets, seeds to plant, puzzles, and always a new book or two. The sense of anticipation is huge. The almost four year old will learn to ride a new bike, the six year old wants to play games and read books. The younger ones relish the excitement of playing with each other, of being together. Parents are busy planning a back-country hiking trip, a rafting outing, bike rides. Play is a principal theme here—we, all of us, are eager to play together.

We have waited a long time for the playfulness of summer, its long sun-drenched days so full of promise. Those feelings on the last day of school before the beginning of summer vacation—that blissful sense of freedom and anticipation centered on the weeks of play just ahead—are impossible to forget. For those of us who now look back several decades to our own childhoods, remembering all the ways we played as children seems magical: neighborhood games played until the sun had set and our parents began calling us home; rigging up kites, working hard to catch the wind and experience the thrill of feeling it soar so high above us; playing endless variations of "house" with siblings and cousins; bike rides and time spent playing on the beach looking for shiny, scurrying rock crabs and treasured agates. Such pleasure! So much delight!

Play *is* magical. It is part of God's creative gift of life helping us use our imaginations to bask in the pleasure, energy, and delight of coming together to play. Sometimes we adults take life so seriously that we forget the freeing sense of play. We refer to people who seem not to have forgotten play's importance as being in their "second childhood." No matter our age, play and playfulness help us delight in one another and in the creative liveliness that play always prompts. Laughter and a spirit of freedom and spontaneity are often side benefits of play, surely signs of God's presence and pleasure in us.

My friend tells a story about her young daughter gathering scraps of colorful material from her mother's sewing basket. Taking the long ribbons of vibrant cloth outside, the little one wanders to the back of the garden where she finds a thin wooden branch and begins attaching the scraps of cloth to the pole with sticky wads of tape. As her mother watches, she begins to bob and dance around the back yard holding high the long branch, the ribbons of cloth rising and falling in the wind. As she weaves precariously around the shrubs and trees, she calls out to her mother, "See?! I'm making a procession so God will come and dance with us!" Play as prayer? Absolutely!

A long-time custom in the Greek Orthodox church is gathering together on Easter Monday to tell jokes. It may seem a bit odd to us, picturing Christians trading jokes. But perhaps we've forgotten that the most extravagant "joke" of all takes place at Easter when even death is defeated and Christ rises from a dark tomb to bring new life and the joy of resurrection. To mark Jesus' victory over death, Orthodox Greeks celebrate the playfulness of surprise, unexpected endings, and humor.

We serious-minded adults would do well to embrace the spiritual practice of play, even thinking of playfulness as the joyful gift it is, a way of being and praying that is life-giving and life affirming. Learning to experience the pleasure of God's presence in playing together, enjoying silliness and the light-hearted freedom of play is both healthy and holy.

Just as summertime includes the joy of play, I look forward to the coming of Christmas when there will be little ones around our table and tree. They will be filled with expectant curiosity, bursting with impatience and eagerly waiting to celebrate and play. I want to learn from them, to join in their silly games, to wrestle and laugh and savor their company. I will remember my own days of child-hood, the making of a manger in the hollow of an old tree-stump, the better to cradle my doll as a newborn. And I will remember my own little daughter, a blue robe wrapped tightly around her to keep out the cold, and her bashful reticence about playing the role of Mary in the school play in the Anglican church across First Turn Road from Wolvercote School in Oxford.

Christ is present in this play—and in *this* play—perhaps even laughing with pleasure with us, the very source of our joy and hap-piness. That's the kind of God we claim, the Holy One who takes our form and comes to us as a child, incarnate, born in a stable! This is the God who loves us and all of creation unconditionally, unreservedly, without strings. This is a God who welcomes and embraces children, telling them they are loved and cherished. Christ is present in every aspect of our lives, including the pleasure of play. Let the games begin!

REFLECTION

We serious-minded adults would do well to embrace the spiritual practice of play, even thinking of playfulness as the joyful gift it is, a way of being and praying that is life-giving and life-affirming. Learning to experience the pleasure of God's presence in playing together, enjoying silliness and the light-hearted freedom of play is both healthy and holy.

- When did you last feel the gift of playfulness? What makes it memorable?

- How might we rethink many different ways of praying so that we see God's presence in the ordinary rhythms of daily life, including play?

- How is play both healthy and holy?

Questing

QUESTING

PERHAPS YOU WILL IDENTIFY with me when I say that I am a person steeped in a religious—particularly Christian—view of the world. Even so, I have spent a good share of my life asking questions, pondering the mysteries, wrestling with the incongruities, and trying to make sense of a religious and theological world that often seems archaic and out of step with twenty-first-century realities. I know I am not alone in this lifelong quest for God. Living for several years in England, many of our neighbors, our friends, the children with whom our daughters played were practicing Muslims, devout Jews, serious Hindus. As Christians, we could not claim a corner on the truth. We could not hammer down a final, cock-sure confession of faith or belief that ignored or dismissed another's experience of the sacred. Our quest required fresh eyes, attentive ears, a willingness to listen and learn and honor other ways of knowing God.

Anyone who has spent time with little ones knows that among the first words a child learns is the question, why? To almost any request or explanation, little children will ask again and again, "Why, Mama?" "Why, Daddy?" From a very young age, we are creatures filled with questions. Why? seems to be universal language for our common longing to make sense of things. The why's of childhood help form a foundation for lifelong questing and our shared search for meaning and purpose, fulfillment, wholeness. In a classic book called *Quest for God*, Rabbi Abraham Joshua Heschel writes beautifully about our longing to know God. Reading it early in my adult years, I found Heschel's poetic words comforting in my own never-ending search—my quest—for God.

Questing is a spiritual practice, a way of praying and being. For many, it can be a daily reality as we seek to understand ourselves and the mysteries of God's presence. Heschel's image that I have carried all these years is of God resting on our eyelids. In the midst of the ordinariness of our lives, God is there whether we feel it or believe it or not. God gives us a spirit of questing, a desire for understanding. Perhaps our questing is not so much for answers about faith and life as it is a process of unearthing mystery. Perhaps God is not so much a conveyor of answers as a cause for wonder?

The word *quest* comes from a Latin root, *quaerere*, which means to seek. No matter our age, our days are filled with questing: "Why, Mommy?" "What does this mean, Grandpa?" "Will I be able to find a meaningful job?" "What will I do when my Parkinson's Disease becomes unmanageable?" "Where will we go when we can't afford to stay in our home?" "Why has cancer taken the lives of so many people I love?" "Where are you, God?" "Why, God?" "How, God?"

Questing stretches our minds and our souls. It's a way of acknowledging our dependence and our lack of certainty about so much of life. It helps us make more of ourselves and more of life. It makes us human. Sometimes at the beginning of a new year, we set aside some time to think intentionally about what we'd like to accomplish, what goals we might set for ourselves. Perhaps we plan for a trip or consider learning something new. We might make lists of things we'd like to achieve or projects we're hoping to complete. Whether as a New Year's resolution or regular wrestling with questions of faith and life, I want to make questing for God part of my daily habit.

My friend, Helen, now in her nineties, has been a "quester" all her life. Blessed with good health, she's an accomplished musician, a gardener and grower of grapes and thus a wine maker, a vibrant presence in her church community, and a lifelong learner. Because she has a curious mind and spirit, she finds joy in learning new things. Helen's eyes shine with interest in others, with gratitude, with grace. She doesn't have life all figured out. Her life isn't perfect and she lives with the usual frustrations and worries that plague us all. But people love to be around her. Her quest for a meaningful life shapes each day—she doesn't know the meaning of boredom. I want to be like her!

Questing and searching for meaning is a spiritual practice. A curious mind and a willingness to ask questions in order to learn new things is a gift. Yes, questing is prayer. As a young person grappling with issues of faith and life—pondering the mysteries, wrestling with the incongruities—my mother had the grace to assure her always-questioning daughter that doubts and questions were healthy signs of a lively mind. May each of us learn to live as questers on a pilgrimage, a journey with God and with one another. May we be willing to explore and question, doubt and wonder. May we learn humility, trusting God in the absence of certainty about God, openly curious and able to hear perspectives different from our own. And may we find in our questing the joy of curiosity and sense of mystery that characterize the spirit of God and a life worth living. Perhaps God is not so much a conveyor of answers as a cause for wonder?

REFLECTION

Questing is a spiritual practice, a way of praying and being. For many, it can be a daily reality as we seek to understand ourselves and the mysteries of God's presence.

- How willing are you to explore and question, doubt and wonder?

- Why does questing or questioning matters of faith sometimes make us uneasy?

- Do you know persons of faith who share their doubts, their own grappling with issues of faith? How do you react to this?

- Name someone you know whose life seems to reflect curiosity and the spiritual practice of questing.

- What do you make of the question, "Perhaps God is not so much a conveyor of answers as a cause for wonder?"

Reverence

Reverence

IN THE WEEKS LEADING from winter into spring, I am keenly aware of slightly longer days and the slow warming of the earth, of budding trees and the gradual greening so longed for in the deep of winter. Finally the cold and seemingly endless darkness of wintertime begins to give way to new life. As earth reawakens from her long night's sleep, one literally can smell the fecundity of the soil and feel the stirring of new life. Where I live, newly hatched salmon have begun long journeys downriver through multiple dams and locks, making their circuitous passage out to the sea. Last fall, we watched mature fish—four or five years old—return over the same routes, swimming against the hard current, climbing fish ladders upstream as they labored to wend their way home to spawn a new generation before dying in the very rivers that gave them life. Long skeins of melodious geese fly north again, their symphony of song and laser-sharp attention to previously traveled routes and familiar nesting grounds another reminder of mysteries we don't begin to understand. In spring the promise of new life, of rebirth and resurrection, is dramatic cause for reverence and wonder.

Together with Saint Francis of Assisi, a thirteenth-century monk who revered nature and all living things, we stand in awe over the astounding presence of God in the world around us. Abandoning wealth and a life of privilege, Saint Francis lived a simple life dedicated to making peace, sharing love for all God's creatures, practicing reverence, and responding to the wonder and sacredness of the whole of creation. This monk's very life was a form of prayer.

Reverence for one another and for the ten thousand things in each of our lives that are ordinary, sometimes even inconsequential, is sometimes more challenging. This year the world has witnessed again a wave of refugees whose faces tell stories of tragedy and loss no one should have to endure. In our own country, the deep injustices of racism, economic disparity, and class discrimination continue to threaten the fabric of this democracy. Some elected leaders show open disdain for programs to support the poor or benefit the common good. Care of our fragile planet still evokes skepticism.

Reverence for every human life should be innate, the position we assume as people created in God's own image—for our own sakes and for the sake of the world. Goethe, a German poet and playwright, thought reverence the "soul of the Christian tradition." Respect for all things, living and non-living, is found in all religious traditions as a fundamental human attribute, a way of showing respect and honoring all that God creates.

In the spirit of Saint Francis, his namesake Pope Francis shows us again and again what it means to have reverence for each other, for the earth, and for the ten thousand things that are part of our everyday lives. "See the faces," Pope Francis reminds us as he avoids power and pomp to spend time with the hungry, the poor, the outcast. Then using his power, he exhorts us to welcome the refugees, show mercy to one another, make places at our own tables for those without tables, and actively engage in caring for the world God has given us.

Saint Francis asks God to make us instruments of peace, sowers of love in the face of hatred, pardoners where there is injury, keepers of faith where there is doubt, bringers of hope in the face of despair, light bearers in the dark places of life, celebrators of joy in the midst of sadness, singers of life. Saint Francis reverences life by reminding us to console, to understand, to love. He reminds us that in giving we receive, in pardoning we are pardoned, and in dying we are born to new life.

Reverence conveys grace and respect regardless of intrinsic value, status, or station. It helps us show regard and support for refugees half a world away and sometimes right next door. It calls for humility and a spirit of grace. Reverence requires doing justice, loving kindness, walking humbly with God knowing that all things are connected, animate and inanimate, human and divine—that just to *be* is holy.

Saint Francis made no distinction between the sacred and the profane. For him, the rebirth and resurrection of springtime was another doorway into God. When we see the Holy One's fingerprints in the birds of the air and the fish in the sea, we understand the universe and its inhabitants as sacred. We love for its own sake, simply because it is and because all things contribute to the order of the whole. Reverence helps us live with a sense of kinship and mutuality, "seeing the faces." Reverence is profound regard for all that God creates. All ground is holy and practicing reverence is a way of praying.

REFLECTION

Reverence conveys grace and respect regardless of intrinsic value, status, or station . . . reverence is profound regard for all that God creates.

- Describe some of the ways nature and the natural world inspire reverence in you.

- In what ways do you resonate to the statement that reverence for every human life should be innate, the position we assume as people created in God's image—for our own sakes and for the sake of the world?

- How does reverence help us live with a sense of kinship and mutuality?

- Do you believe with Goethe, the German playwright and poet, that reverence is the soul of the Christian tradition? What might this imply?

Stillness

Stillness

In a small, quiet room lit by soft lamp light and the glow of candles—a spare place marked with expectation and a profound sense of the sacred—a group of friends gathers again for conversation and catching up. At the beginning and ending of their time together, there is silence and prayer. And while the conversations and catching up are at the center of their intertwined lives, the silence at the beginning and the prayer at the ending are the bookends providing a rhythm and a pattern that shape and define the group.

We gather at the end of the day to make sense of our lives. We need the comfort and collective wisdom that will help us better know ourselves and the busy worlds we inhabit. We long for peace and the solace of quiet, for the promise of the light of Christ and the assurance of God's Spirit in our midst. We are tired, afraid, in need of healing. And so we set aside the busyness and the chaos to make this space a place to be still.

These friends were part of my life for almost two decades. We shared life-changing illnesses, joys and sorrows, two premature and unforeseen deaths. Our time together was itself life-changing and now, several years later, I still feel the stillness of that quiet room, the silence of God's presence, the palpable peace.

Their voices, their laughter, and the ways each of them brought such richness to our monthly gatherings are inscribed in my heart. I treasure their friendship and their memories. But the stillness we experienced together, so uncharacteristic of the ways we usually interact, is part of the cherished time we shared and a gift I continue to ponder.

Stillness as prayer is powerful. It needs to be guarded and treasured because for most of us silence too often eludes us and very often we avoid it. Sometimes it makes us uncomfortable and we hurry to fill its gaping, undefinable and uneasy presence. Stillness can be frightening. It leaves us seemingly alone and vulnerable, open perhaps to dreaded memories, unattended issues, or hard questions of life and faith.

Words and chatter or busyness mask our uneasiness. Not wanting to let down our guard and clinging to the illusion of being in control, the clamor and din of the world is where we find ourselves more often—sometimes wearily and sometimes by choice. "Be still," my grandmother used to say. "Quiet time," I say to my own grandchildren. Stop the running and the spinning of your life. Rest. Heal. Be.

Making space for stillness—silence—in worship is something many of us long for. That silence may be the only place in the course of a week where God's presence is tangibly touched and tasted. Stillness in worship is a physical experience, an act of grace and mercy, a vessel for listening to the beating of our own hearts and space for hearing the breath that gives us life.

Making space for stillness—silence—in the course of everyday life can also be a place of comfort and peace, space for God. Stillness helps us pay attention and focus. It opens a place for God to speak and be. What has been done has been done. What has not been done has not been done. Let it be.

While non-stop news blares from every corner of the earth, spewing story after endless story of mind-numbing information, we must stop to make space for silence. The barrage of messages and texts and instant communication that assault our senses and rob our spirits must be put on hold. We must listen to the beating heart of the universe, to the silence of our own longings. We must make space for the holy. Our bodies and our minds cannot function effectively without the perspective stillness evokes.

Our culture values productivity and we measure worth by profit and cost. Stillness is sacred space that cannot be measured in the world's terms. Its gift is the quiet of a still small voice. Its gift is that no words are needed. Its gift is the peaceful acknowledgment that we can simply be still. We can simply *be*.

Perhaps stillness is the *best* definition of prayer. Standing still, being still, tearing away all the masks we wear and all the words we share, we open ourselves to God's mysterious care. "Be present, Spirit of God, within us," we pray. "We are your dwelling place and your home. May the darkness of our lives be penetrated by your light. May our troubles be calmed by your peace. May all evil be redeemed by Christ's love, all pain transformed by Christ's suffering, and all dying glorified in the risen life of Christ." Let us be still in the presence of God. Holy ground indeed!

REFLECTION

Their voices, their laughter, and the ways each of them brought such richness to our monthly gatherings are inscribed in my heart. I treasure their friendship and their memories. But the stillness we experienced together, so uncharacteristic of the ways we usually interact, is part of the cherished time we shared and a gift I continue to ponder.

- Describe a place or a time when you truly experience stillness.

- In what ways are you tired, afraid, or in need of healing?

- We long for peace and the solace of quiet, for the promise of the light of Christ and the assurance of God's Spirit in our midst. Why is it so hard for us to embrace stillness?

- The psalmist's admonition to be still and know that I am God is a mantra for many. What are some ways you might make this a daily prayer?

- Perhaps stillness is the *best* definition of prayer. Standing still, being still, tearing away all the masks we wear and all the words we share, we open ourselves to God's mysterious care. Yes? Maybe? No?

Thanksgiving

Thanksgiving

It isn't surprising that Americans sometimes tout the holiday of Thanksgiving as a favorite. Coming as it does late in the fall, our thanks on Thanksgiving is a collective sigh of gratitude for the gifts of fields and gardens, memories of the long warm days of summer that brought such pleasure and produced food in abundance, perhaps a heightened awareness of the privileges of living in this land we call home, and maybe even some relief as the days grow short and we begin to "batten down the hatches" in preparation for winter.

This quiet holiday that embodies thanksgiving and focuses on blessings seems to convey goodwill and relaxed appreciation. There aren't a lot of expectations. We simply gather together to acknowledge the fact that we are guests on this earth and the fortunate recipients of its good gifts. Families seem to meet with less baggage and a spirit of—well, thanksgiving!—for one another and for the simple joys of belonging together. There aren't the complications of gift buying or what may seem like the responsibilities of decorating our homes. We buy our fat butter-basted turkeys, stuff and roast them in anticipation of the feast around a table laden with other traditional fall food, and then in the stupor of having eaten more than usual, we relax to play games or take a walk, watch football, and enjoy one another's company.

For many, the thanks that characterizes this American holiday feels authentic, an honest recognition of our dependence and good fortune. There is a notable spirit of generosity, hospitality, gratitude, and goodwill. Thanksgiving and yes, thanksgiving—seems to bring out the best in us, prompting generosity and kindness for those whose tables may not be filled with so much good food, the conversation of family, or even much hope. And of course thanksgiving is a life-long practice, one we sometimes need to cultivate and nurture and not simply honor as a holiday.

Living with an attitude of thanksgiving is to practice the art of prayer. The grace of gratitude is infectious, a reminder of the goodness of God and a contagious nod to living joyfully and generously. In its embodiment of God's generosity and grace, thanksgiving—gratitude—also exacts of us responsibility for others, holding us to the fire to *be* grace, to *be* compassion, to understand and respond to the needs of our neighbor and the needs of the world. It's a way of life, a stance, an attitude—a way of acknowledging our common humanity. And in this way, thanksgiving implies an outwardness of generosity as we bear Christ's love, God's grace, beyond ourselves.

Sometimes thanksgiving is crowded out by boredom or despair or self-absorption. Rather than giving thanks for the wonder of each new day, for the rising of the sun and the life-giving waters of rain and snow, we fret over the myriad worries and wants that characterize our inability simply to be grateful. Looking at what isn't instead of what is can be a bottomless well of unhappiness and misery. Without being trite, it truly is about seeing a glass half full. The very grammar of thanksgiving and gratitude is life-giving.

A central component to weekly worship is the Great Thanksgiving. Eucharist is another word for thanksgiving. The people who gather and the presider who celebrates the gifts of bread and wine are offering thanks together, praying the table prayer. *The Lord be with you . . . And also with you . . . Lift up your hearts . . . We lift them to the Lord . . . Let us give thanks to the Lord our God . . . It is right to give our thanks and praise.*

Eucharisteo—thanksgiving—always precedes the miracle that we are fed and nourished at the table of the Lord. I like to think of us as guests at that table—the good earth—with God as host. And in spite of our short-sightedness or forgetfulness, the gifts of God never stop flowing: daily breath that gives us life, food and drink, companionship, and this wondrously generative earth we call home.

Saying thank you is a primary act of good manners. It's one of the first things we teach young children. Thanksgiving is a way of living that focuses on all that comes to us without merit and without strings attached, whether we ask for it or not. Living with an intentional attitude of thanksgiving helps us see the world through a lens of gratitude. One medieval Christian mystic, Meister Eckhart, wrote centuries ago that if the only prayer we ever say is *thank you*, that is enough. May we learn to live with the art of gratitude and the grace of thanksgiving.

REFLECTION

Thanksgiving is a way of living that focuses on all that comes to us without our asking, without merit, and without strings attached. Living with an intentional attitude of thanksgiving helps us see the world through a lens of gratitude.

- Why does thanksgiving seem to bring out the best in us?

- Name some ways you practice thanksgiving.

- How do you experience thanksgiving in the Eucharist?

- What are some ways you celebrate the Thanksgiving holiday in your home?

Unity

Unity

IN THESE FIRST DECADES of the twenty-first century, we've born a heavy load of the "us and them" mentality. Neighbors against neighbors, communities against communities, religions against religions, nations against nations—it reads all too painfully like so many Old Testament prophesies. Add to this the hyperbole of several seasons of political elections and the harsh, even mean spirit of misinformed patriotism and polarizing political voices that seek to divide rather than unify. Walls and borders, enemies and adversaries, separation and division. A heavy load indeed!

But there are other points of view too. One of those views is an image many of us will recall from the days of the Apollo space missions. It was the first time that the trajectory of the moon mission made possible a picture of the earth from outer space. That poignantly beautiful photograph of our common home evoked a sense of awe, oneness, and unity. There was no "us and them"—we all shared mutual claim to this remarkable planet. The astronauts floating deep in space told of their own existential awakenings, their own sense of oneness and connectedness as they viewed their unforgettable world from such a distance.

As scientific discoveries continue to unlock the mysteries of the universe, this new cosmology illustrates even more poignantly the biblical assertion that unity is the Holy One's desire and is indeed the pattern of the universe. The new universe story embraces an ever-expanding cosmos without fixed borders and boundaries or static beginnings and endings, of connectedness that can serve to unite us all *for it is the story of us all.* This "new" science continues to change radically the ways we think about our planet and the story of creation, making connections that seem to share a lot in common with the language of mystics and poets. No longer is it possible to see ourselves as separate and disconnected from others. We know ourselves to be part of this ever-expanding, generative explosion of life and matter.

Jesus' fundamental unity with God defined his ministry together with calling his followers to that same radical unity. Unity seems to be God's vision, God's intention. References to relationality and oneness are common biblical themes. Fourteenth-century German theologian and mystic Meister Eckhart taught relationality as the essence of everything that is, the handwork of the Holy One.

If we are to survive the myriad social and ecological problems of our day, we must get over our delusions of separateness—better than, smarter than, more powerful than—to recognize our common need for one another, for our earth home, and the universe that connects us all. We must put away our arrogance and desire to dominate and instead find unity in diversity, mutual humility, and the wholeness of communion and community—unity as an act of prayer.

Closer to home, our own holy ground, we know that in spite of all the diversity and differences between living and non-living things, there is a web of unity and interconnectedness that belies those differences. So sensitive is our interrelatedness that the tiny atmospheric changes caused by the flap of a butterfly's wings can later have major effects on the course of our weather—a butterfly flapping its wings in South America can affect the weather in New York's Central Park. This "butterfly effect" shows a fantastically complex web of connections that we don't begin to comprehend.

We need one another. We need the unity of our shared humanity and our common story as we seek to make the world a better place. We need to care for our fragile planet and the multitude of creatures that make it such a remarkable example of God's handiwork. Unity in the midst of so much diversity is an affirmation, a prayer acknowledging all that we share in common and all the ways we depend on one another.

Today as I write, rain splatters against my window, individual drops seeking each other out and coming together in rivulets of water that nourish the trees and shrubs around my home and eventually feed into a nearby creek and then into a large river . . . Today as I write, I listen to the music of a mass choir, the unity of their voices combining with the sounds of all the instruments in the accompanying orchestra to make sounds so complex and rich that I join my voice to theirs to make music together . . . Today as I write alone in my study, I am connected to each of you as we share our common need for mutuality and wholeness, compassion and justice.

We share kinship, you and I, and a common stake in the survival of our own souls and of Mother Earth. We are integrally connected to one another and to a vast and ever-expanding cosmos that has no boundaries, no borders. Our life-giving and life-affirming words and actions are marks of wholeness and resurrection, part of the saving acts of God. Unity and harmony are sacred ways of being, the underlying truth of all things, God's intention, and prayer itself. We will flourish and our planet will flourish if we can learn to embrace wholeness and holy acts of unity, respect and regard, dignity and compassion for ourselves and for all creation.

REFLECTION

If we are to survive the myriad social and ecological problems of our day, we must get over our delusions of separateness—better than, smarter than, more powerful than—to recognize our common need for one another, for our earth home, and the universe that connects us all. We must put away our arrogance and desire to dominate to find unity in diversity, mutual humility, and the wholeness of communion and community—unity as an act of prayer.

Unity

- What does it mean to you that unity and harmony are sacred ways of being, the underlying truth of all things, God's intention, and prayer itself?

- Name some ways you notice webs of unity and interconnectedness.

- How is unity different from uniformity?

- Spend some time reading about the new cosmology. One source for non-scientists is Judy Cannato's *Radical Amazement*.

VISION

Vision

"I HAVE A DREAM . . . that one day this nation will rise up and live out the true meaning of its creed . . . I have a dream that one day justice will roll down like waters and righteousness like a mighty stream . . . I have a dream!" These words and their passionate cadence, so familiar to all of us, are more than prophetic words, more than a call to action, more than a famous speech. With urgency and fervent hope, they proclaim Martin Luther King's ardent vision for a world where justice reigns and freedom rolls down like the life-giving river it is—for all God's children.

Vision as prayer? Oh yes! Martin Luther King is part of a long line of visionaries calling us "to loose the bonds of injustice, undo the thongs of the yoke, and let the oppressed go free." Visionaries practice the art of seeing what may be invisible, what many have long since given up on, what cynics refuse even to consider. Vision helps us know what to stand for and it gives us a moral compass. With invitations and admonishments, Jesus—another prophet and visionary—illustrated again and again what it means to be God's partners in a vision to transfigure the world.

In this twenty-first century, we still live in a world polarized by fear and anxiety. Divisive and combative voices and an endless barrage of contentious issues too often drown out the words of leaders and dreamers like Martin Luther King. We seem to lack a vision for the common good and the will to stand for the things we value most. Civility in public discourse and sometimes in private conversation is painfully lacking. In the midst of this simmering cauldron of vengeance and anger and discord, we are charged with a different vision: "This is what YHWH asks of you, to act justly, to love tenderly, and to walk humbly with your God." God calls us to be pain-bearers, life-givers, peace-makers, visionaries. God's vision is always about justice and peace and it always leads us into the midst of human suffering.

Vision as prayer? Oh yes! Vision means seeing the hidden good, not giving up hope, refusing to be cynical, practicing the art of seeing what may be obscure. Vision is a glimmer of hope for all the things that make for a just and peaceful world. Vision has to do with what we most value, what we find important in life, and what will make us better people and our world a better place. Vision is about renewal and wisdom and a yearning for the common good.

Worship and liturgy show us a vision of God's dream. We come together on the Sabbath to remember who we are, to lament and pray, hope and sing. All are welcome. Confessions are made, blessings given, peace offered. Bread is broken and wine is poured so all might be fed. Communion implies unity, empathy, community—it's a vision for the world, an invitation to make space for everyone, to imagine our best selves and our highest hopes. In worship and liturgy, we are sent out to feed and care for others. In worship we practice the reign of God here and now: a vision of grace for a world where everyone is fed, forgiven, loved.

Vision as prayer? Oh yes! Read modern-day visionaries like Dorothy Day, Jim Wallis, Joan Chittister, Desmond Tutu, Munib Younan. Their words and their lives witness to radical, visionary faith. They remind us that we ignore at our peril a wounded world where poverty and hunger breed war and terror. They inspire us to be vessels for bearing God's reign of justice and peace. They give us courage to imagine and act and they show us how to be the hands and face of Christ. They know that in carrying out God's work in the world we become Christ's very body, a vision for transforming the world into God's true home.

Christianity and many other faith traditions affirm that *we* are made in God's image. What a vision for calling *us* to be visionary and for cultivating the art of seeing the invisible. What a reason for being! Knowing ourselves to be made in God's image empowers us and gives us purpose to act and dream and embody God's vision. Being a visionary is at the heart of Christianity. It is about practicing the reign of God here and now. Vision as prayer? Oh yes!

REFLECTION

Visionaries practice the art of seeing what may be invisible, what many have long since given up on, what cynics refuse even to consider. Vision helps us know what to stand for and it gives us a moral compass. With invitations and admonishments, Jesus—another prophet and visionary—illustrated again and again what it means to be God's partners in a vision to transfigure the world.

- Take time to think about visionaries you admire and have learned from—who are they and how have they shaped your view of the world?

- Describe some ways worship functions as a vision for enacting the reign of God.

- Consider the ways that vision means seeing the hidden good, not giving up hope, refusing to be cynical, and practicing the art of seeing what may be obscure.

Wonder

WONDER

THE EXTRAORDINARY DISCOVERY OF gravitational waves by astronomers only a short while ago captures my imagination. Heralded as the beginning of a new era in astrophysics, this discovery of vibrations in space and time means that we now can hear the cosmos as well as see it. And while I'm hardly an astrophysicist and certainly not a scientist, I stop in wonder over a discovery that allows us a whole new way of experiencing the universe.

I've sometimes written about the place of my childhood. It is holy ground for me, a stunningly beautiful part of the Pacific Northwest where tree-covered islands and saltwater inlets are shaped by daily tides, their beaches strewn with odd assortments of driftwood and logs, shells and agates, and endless varieties of salt-water creatures. It's the place where I first began to wonder about the mysteries of the universe. Perhaps I thought I could hear the cosmos in the steady ebb and flow of the tides. Perhaps God's presence was more tangible here because every day was filled with a sense of wonder.

With the coming of night and the vast canopy of the star-studded heavens holding us in thrall, that sense of wonder is stirred again—an overwhelming curiosity about the God who creates and orders the universe and our place in its infinite vastness. I knew—then and now—that wonder is prayer and that we are co-creators with this mysterious God who seemingly without effort flings stars and planets across the heavens and creates sea creatures and human creatures and every living thing.

Nature and the boundary-less universe around us are ever-changing exhibits of wonder and mystery. As scientists continue to probe the far reaches of our tiny solar system into the galaxies beyond—now even listening to the sounds of gravitational waves as they circulate in wide spirals of musical notes, we're invited to embrace the unknown. Who is this God who tells us (together with Job) to gird up our loins and take notice of the handiwork that can be heard and seen everywhere we look? Who is this God who reminds us that our lives matter and that we ourselves are God-bearers, called to be the hands and face of Christ, bearing God's goodness to one another and to the earth that is our home? Who is this God who continues to create, continues to love, whose very essence is generativity and grace?

Writer and theologian Frederick Buechner invites readers to listen to their lives. Where are the places of wonder in your life, in your world? Where do you go to be still, to listen? In the chaos of political tragedy in our own country, many of us carry a heavy load of worry and the weight of helplessness and anger as we watch freedom undermined, leadership abused, and our nation reeling in disarray. Wonder seems a luxury for better times, an extravagance we can't afford in dark days. How do we stop the interminable voices and the groundswell of news to make room for the wonder and silence of prayer? How do we listen to our lives? How do we hear?

As I write, I turn off the incessant noise to listen to a tiny hummingbird flitting among the flowers hanging outside my window. The sound of its wings is unmistakable. I watched this delicate creature (or one just like it) when it first "flew the coop", making the leap from its miniature nest the size of a quarter to begin a life journey that includes yearly migrations I can't even imagine. Watching these elusive little birds whose astonishing sense of memory includes knowing every flower in their territory and how long it takes for each to refill with nectar fills me with a sense of wonder and amazement as do so many other creatures that grace us with their presence—truly wonders of creation.

And yet we seem always to be looking for ways to parse the limits of God's presence and power. We want to define and categorize and carve in stone that which is beyond our wildest imaginings, things we don't begin to comprehend. We can't imagine love so vast and deep and complete as to know no limits. We don't begin to fathom the imagination of God. This universe is a light and sound show of the generativity of God. It knows no bounds, there are no limits, and it is God's home.

But wonder of wonders, we too are God's home. We have been made in the image of God and are charged with sharing the infinite and unutterable love of God shown to us in the world we call home. We are part of the wonder of a universe filled with sight *and* sound, offering us glimpses of God wherever we turn. This God rests on our eyelids and lives in each of us—wonder of wonders!

REFLECTION

I knew—then and now—that wonder is prayer and that we are co-creators with this mysterious God who seemingly without effort flings stars and planets across the heavens and creates sea creatures and human creatures and every living thing.

- Where are the places of wonder in your life, in your world? Describe a time or a place where you feel (or felt) a sense of wonder. Notice how the memory affects you.

- Where do you go to be still, to listen?

- What might it mean that we are co-creators with God, that we are God's home?

- How does nature and the natural world elicit a sense of wonder for you?

- How do you define wonder? Wonder as prayer?

X as mystery

X as mystery

A LOVELY QUOTE I sometimes share on the occasion of birthdays—artfully written in calligraphy—captures something of the mystery of each of our lives: "Suddenly all my ancestors are behind me. 'Be still,' they say. 'Watch and listen. You are the result of the love of thousands.'" We often use the letter X to symbolize what we do not know or cannot understand—the unknown. When I contemplate the long, circuitous line of my own ancestors—each of us conceived in love—I can barely imagine the mystery of my own *being* let alone the Great Unknown at the center of the universe, the creator God.

Perhaps age and the accumulated experiences of six going on seven decades of life play a role in embracing mystery and what we do not understand. But I am captivated by how the language of some scientists involved in new understandings of the universe sounds so much like the language of the mystics. Contemplating the grains of sand on a beach as a way of comprehending the size of a boundary-less universe or thinking about the mysteries of our own existence or the conviction that God took human form in the person of Jesus are examples of the Great Unknown.

It isn't that I want to bask in the fog of all that we do not know. But I find this X as mystery—symbolic for a God we cannot define—enormously liberating and compelling. It reminds us that we are part of something so much bigger than ourselves and it grounds us here on earth while transporting us far beyond the tiny place we occupy in the universe. And it cannot help but make us humble. What immeasurable love! What generosity and grace! What a source of joy and comfort to know *and not know* the presence and the mystery of a God we simply cannot nail down however hard we try.

For me and perhaps for you, the liturgy of the church helps illumine the Great Unknown, this God who comes to dwell with us.

> *We give you thanks, O God, for in the beginning your Spirit moved over the waters and by your Word you created the world, calling forth life in which you took delight. I am the Bread of life; you who come to me shall not hunger. Eat this bread, drink this cup, taste and see the goodness of God. Now the green blade rises from the buried grain . . . Love is come again like wheat arising green. Now the feast and celebration, all of creation sings for joy . . . to the God of life and love and freedom, praise and glory forever more.*

Poets and artists and mystics are good at helping us grasp something of the mystery of life on this planet. They seem to know inherently that matters of faith are not nailed-down certitudes or verifiable facts but processes and practices, fluid and complex amalgamations of understanding that help illumine what cannot be defined. Their ability to use words and images, to explain with metaphor and allegory and symbol, with parables and fables and tales that captivate and mystify, is part of the process. God gives us a spirit of questing, a hunger for unraveling the mysteries.

In an earlier reflection, I describe an unforgettable experience on a high mountain pass one dark summer night. It was August and "as midnight approached and the light of the western sky turned completely dark, our own Milky Way Galaxy began to show its unfathomable size and beauty just overhead. Through telescopes, we could see other galaxies including Andromeda as well as dying stars and 'shooting stars' and stars just being born. Most of all, we gazed with wonder at the heavens above us and at the stars and planets and galaxies that silently blossomed across the fields of the night sky. In the stillness and awe of that night, we truly understood the earth to be in heaven."

In no way was this simply a lesson in astronomy or even a way of recognizing the wonders of the cosmos, though it was both of these. It was X as mystery, a mind-blowing experience of what is not rational or measurable or able to be grasped—the infinite and vast beauty of an ever-expanding universe without borders or limits and an accompanying uneasy awareness of our own enigmatic character—at once familiar and unfamiliar, verifiable but mysterious, connected and unconnected.

Our notions of God are too small and there is so much we do not know. And yet the dark Mystery at the heart of the universe continues to connect us and all things, animate and inanimate. We are part of a whole and each of us—profound mystery ourselves—is made in the image of this God, carried by God's spirit, imbued with God's very breath. "Listen to your life," says Frederick Buechner. "See it for the fathomless mystery it is." Consider that long line of ancestors whose lives are intertwined with yours. Consider a God both hidden and revealed, a God who comes to dwell with us to make us God's own people, a God who makes all things new. This is X as mystery, the Great Unknown beating heart at the center of the universe as well as the Holy One at the center of our own beating hearts. X as mystery inspires wordless prayer and the language of silence—mysterious gifts indeed!

REFLECTION

It isn't that I want to bask in the fog of all that we do not know. But I find this X as mystery—symbolic for a God we cannot define— enormously liberating and compelling. It inspires awe and wonder. It reminds us that we are part of something so much bigger than ourselves. It grounds us here on earth while transporting us far beyond the tiny place we occupy in the universe.

- Take time to consider the following: X marks the mystery of a living God. Each of us—profound mystery ourselves—is made in the image of this God, carried by God's spirit, imbued with God's very breath. We are made whole—resurrected, renewed, restored—by the God of life. Each of our lives is filled with mystery and Mystery.

- What are the challenges in living with mystery?

Yearning

Yearning

Newly settled in a large city, we'd found a church with an interesting website and a reputation for ecumenical partnering—not just any partnering, but an established, twenty-plus-year-old parish serving both Lutherans and Catholics. So on a warm Sunday morning in September, still feeling a bit disheveled from the recent move and missing our "old" and familiar place of worship, we set off to find this community.

An undistinguished sign along the road and a nearly full parking lot should have been clues. Finding a space to park, we walked suspiciously alone up the curving sidewalk accompanied by loud and exuberant singing pouring from open windows: "Christ, be our light! Shine in our hearts. Shine through the darkness. Christ, be our light! Shine in your church gathered today."[1] We slipped into the nearest pew noting several turned heads and sets of eyes watching with amusement and quickly joined our voices to theirs: "Longing for peace, our world is troubled, longing for hope, many despair . . . Longing for shelter, many are homeless, longing for warmth, many are cold. Make us your building, sheltering others, walls made of living stone."

The yearning in their voices was palpable and the longing in our hearts an ache—the familiarity of the hauntingly beautiful hymn about justice and peace, a gathering of unfamiliar faces, the belonging and the not belonging. And just as we'd ratcheted up a few volumes more of "Christ, be our light," it was over. The closing

1. Farrel, "Christ, Be Our Light."

hymn bookmarked the end of worship. Slightly embarrassed, we shook a few hands, heard apologies for the church's incorrect worship time on their website and church sign, and accepted sheepish invitations to come back an hour earlier next week.

The yearning remained. "Longing for light, we wait in darkness. Longing for truth, we turn to you. Make us your own, your holy people, light for the world to see . . ." For us of course, it was the missed experience of Sabbath worship, the desire for being connected to a community, and an uneasy sense of being in a time warp and unfamiliar with the lay of the land.

For this Lutheran-Catholic parish, the yearning is a two-decades-long affirmation of being the body of Christ together. Their yearning is a weekly witness to embrace one another and all who long for God's face together with making a home for Lutherans and Catholics in spite of the separations of 500 years. They long for unity and they have created an extraordinary model for re-membering the body of Christ.

We visited again a few weeks later. The priest, reading from a text about the woman at the well, spoke longingly in his sermon about the transformative power of women's stories. Observers could have heard a pin drop as this usually clamorous congregation listened intently to a double-edged homily so filled with irony and truth. A pianist who happened to be Sikh was filling in that Sunday. Wearing his Sikh turban proudly, he accompanied a rousing liturgy—". . . for peace in the world, for the health of the church, for the unity of all, . . . for peace in our hearts, for peace in our homes . . . let us pray to the Lord!"[2] And then at a table hosted by a female Lutheran pastor and a male Catholic priest, we received the bread and wine of the Eucharist. I cannot think of this without a catch in my throat. The profound sense of yearning, unity, and genuine joy so palpable in that gathered body of worshipers that autumn morning was breathtaking.

All of creation seems to yearn for wholeness. Biblical writers, poets, and musicians often capture our common yearnings in words and images and song—describing the whole creation

2. Liturgy from *Evangelical Lutheran Worship*.

groaning together like a woman in childbirth struggling to birth new life. Even among skeptics and perhaps even die-hard cynics, I believe there is a deeply buried longing to be part of something bigger than ourselves, a yearning to be whole. Christians profess faith in the Holy One who embodies wholeness and fullness, the resurrected Christ who makes all things new restoring creation and all created things into what God intended from the beginning.

We too groan for new life. We too yearn to be whole. This longing is part of our very nature, an impulse and sense of completeness found in love and in Love. We are made in God's image. We are made for life together and for unity with God. What seems to be an inherent predisposition—this innate knowing that we are made for life together and for unity with God—is a gift, a reminder that God's love and grace is enough, that God's love and grace make love and grace of us, that God's love and grace make us truly whole. And it is the cause of our yearning—prayer indeed!

> Many the gifts, many the people, many the hearts that yearn to belong. Let us be servants to one another, making your kingdom come . . . Christ, be our light! Shine in our hearts. Shine through the darkness.

REFLECTION

All of creation seems to yearn for wholeness. Even in skeptics and perhaps even in die-hard cynics, I believe there is a deeply buried longing to be part of something bigger than ourselves, a yearning to be whole.

- How is this yearning to be whole demonstrated in daily life?

- Name a time or an occasion in your life when you felt this kind of longing for God.

- How would you describe yearning as prayer?

Zeal

Zeal

A COUPLE OF CHRISTMASES ago, my youngest daughter—very pregnant with her first child—and her spouse came home to celebrate with us. We had only a few days together but she wanted to make some meals that could be frozen in preparation for after the baby's birth. Before they arrived, I stocked up on zip-lock bags and plastic containers in anticipation of making meatballs or spaghetti sauce or other simple meals that could be frozen easily.

Megan arrived with a very large box. In it were *all* the spices from her pantry, various kinds of vinegar and oil, fresh ginger and cloves of garlic, colorful peppers, two or three cookbooks, and many other ingredients for making gourmet freezer meals. This daughter of mine whose passion for good food began at an early age was not interested in ordinary spaghetti or Swedish meatballs. Her zeal for creating extraordinarily interesting meals meant that smells of curry and ginger and garlic wafted through our house for days. She was celebrating an impending birth by creating meals worthy of so momentous a milestone.

I relish this light-hearted example about a beloved daughter. But as I write today, I want to think more substantively about what it means to practice zeal. We inhabit a world fueled by creative, generative energy. We are surrounded by inspiring people, like former president Jimmy Carter, now in his nineties, still passionate about issues of justice and fairness, still building homes for Habitat for Humanity. Our world is a better place because of ardent activists like Dorothy Day, the devoted Catholic convert whose commitments to social justice earned her the reputation of "political radical" or the Niebuhr brothers who wrote and spoke so eloquently about the intersections of religion and daily life. The world is better because of zealous people who model compassion and generosity of spirit, who generate joy and love and refuse to succumb to cynicism. Our world is better when we engage with one another, when we help inspire and empower others.

In the midst of our own political upheaval and against the backdrop of an always-conflicted planet, I am grateful for the zeal of journalists and writers and activists who keep us informed and passionate about our own roles and responsibilities. Life is short and we should honor and cherish the wonder and the drama, the ordinary and the extraordinary, the good and the not-so-good. Whether we are passionate "foodies" absorbed with recipes, fascinated with the machinations of politics, invigorated by books and learning, captivated by nature and the natural world, engaged with causes of all kinds, or energized by simplicity and quiet contemplation, living life meaningfully requires passion and zeal.

Passion and zeal are responses to the grace and love of God. Our reaction to God's generosity and generativity can be a way of praying. Brother Lawrence—a seventeenth-century monk whose passion for good food was something like my daughter's—wrote that cooking for him was a way of practicing the presence of God: "... in the noise and clatter of my kitchen, I possess God in as great tranquility as if I were upon my knees [in prayer]."[1]

Life is short and we have only a small window of time to explore the amazing world God has created—the vagaries of politics and religion, the tastes and textures of good food, the astounding beauty of nature, the wonder of human life in all its diversity. Life is short and we all hope to live lives that matter, that make the world a better place. It requires zeal to act for justice, to make peace. It takes passion to give ourselves to the common good, to do our small bit for others, to make a fabulous meal. Nothing is accomplished without passion and zeal.

1. Brussat, *Spiritual Literacy*, 219.

We acknowledge the overwhelming love of God when we share that same love and generosity of spirit for all that God has created. To feel kinship with all people and with all God's creatures regarding others as our sisters, our brothers, is to recognize the Holy. God wants our hearts. Our love and care for this earth we call home expands and enhances our love of the Creator.

My daughter's zeal for cooking is a passion she finds enormously creative and satisfying. Now with two little ones of her own, she often talks with me about a new recipe or a restaurant where the food is "amazing." It's part of her passion for the goodness of life. For me, it's grace and Grace and the joy of family. Today as I savor summer's warm sunshine, take time to write several notes to friends, engage in conversations both mundane and captivating, I am grateful for God's amazing gift of life and the creative, generative energy it inspires.

With philosopher Henri-Frédéric Amiel, we pray with zeal:

> Life is short and we do not have much time to gladden the hearts of those who travel with us. So be swift to love and make haste to be kind and go in peace to love and serve God. Amen.[2]

REFLECTION

Whether we are passionate "foodies" absorbed with recipes, fascinated with the machinations of politics, invigorated by books and learning, captivated by nature and the natural world, engaged with causes of all kinds, or energized by simplicity and quiet contemplation, living life meaningfully requires passion and zeal. Passion and zeal are responses to the grace and love of God.

- What inspires zeal in you? Why?

- Name someone whose passion for life inspires you. What is it like to be around this person?

2. Amiel, *Amiel's Journal*, Dec 16, 1868.

- What do you think it means that the creative, generative energy of the world and its creatures invites individual and communal energy?

- How might our reaction to God's generosity and generativity be a way of praying?

- How does zeal become grace? Prayer?

Resources

Amiel, Henri-Frédéric. *Amiel's Journal*. 1885. Online at www.gutenburg.org.

Bass, Diana Butler. *Grounded: Finding God in the World*. New York: HarperOne, 2015.

Briehl, Susan, and Marty Haugen. *Turn My Heart: A Sacred Journey from Brokenness to Healing*. Chicago: GIA, 2003.

Brussat, Frederic, and Mary Ann Brussat. *Spiritual Literacy: Reading the Sacred in Everyday Life*. New York: Scribner, 1996.

Buechner, Frederick. *Listening to Your Life: Daily Meditation with Frederick Buechner*. New York: Harper Collins, 1996.

Cannato, Judy. *Radical Amazement*. Notre Dame, IN: Sorin, 2006.

Eiseley, Loren. "A Cry of Joy." In *Creative Brooding*, edited by Robert Raines, 124–26. New York: Macmillan, 1967.

Evangelical Lutheran Worship. Minneapolis: Augsburg Fortress, 2006.

Farrell, Bernadette. "Christ, Be Our Light." Hymn. Portland, OR: OCP, 1993.

Heschel, Abraham Joshua. *Quest for God: Studies in Prayer and Symbolism*. New York: Crossroad, 1982.

Lamott, Anne. *Help, Thanks, Wow: The Three Essential Prayers*. New York: Penguin Random House, 2012.

Nelson, Gertrud Mueller. *To Dance with God: Family Ritual and Community Celebration*. Mahwah, NJ: Paulist, 1986.

Rohr, Richard. Center for Action and Contemplation website. https://cac.org.

Saint Teresa of Avila. "Christ Has No Body." Online at www.theworkofthepeople.com.

Schmemann, Alexander. "Fr. Alexander Schmemann on the Need for Joy." Online at www.solzemli.wordpress.com.

———. *The Journals of Father Alexander Schmemann*. Yonkers, NY: St. Vladimir's Seminary, 1983.

Taylor, Barbara Brown. *Learning to Walk in the Dark*. New York: HarperOne, 2014.